Empowered by the Spirit

'You will receive power when the
Holy Spirit comes down on you'
— Acts 1.8

Preparing for
the Sacrament of
Confirmation

William E. Odell

OUR SUNDAY VISITOR PUBLISHING DIVISION

OUR SUNDAY VISITOR, INC.

Huntington, Indiana

Contributing Author: Catherine M. Odell, M.ED.
Project Manager: Charles A. Savitskas, S.T.L.
Consultants: Rev. Terry J. Tekippe, S.T.L., Ph.D., Richard Reichert, M.A., M.R.E.,
          Dennis Beeman, M.Div., Loretta Beeman, B.A., Margaret A. Savitskas, B.A.

Nihil Obstat: ✠John F. Whealon, D.D., S.T.L., S.S.L.
          Archbishop of Hartford
       ✠Lawrence J. Riley, D.D., S.T.D., LL.D.
          Auxiliary Bishop of Boston
       ✠Austin B. Vaughan, D.D.
          Auxiliary Bishop of New York
       Sister M. Jane Carew C.S.J., M.A., M.Div., D.Min.
       Rev. Walter J. Edyvean, S.T.D.
       Rev. John T. Ford, C.S.C., S.T.D.
       Rev. John Hardon, S.J., M.A., S.T.D.
       Rev. Richard P. Hire, M.A., M.Div.
       Rev. Ronald Lawler, O.F.M. Cap., Ph.D.
       Rev. James T. O'Connor, S.T.D.
       Rev. Val J. Peter, S.T.L., S.T.D., J.C.D.
       Rev. John Sheets, S.J., S.T.L., S.T.D.

Imprimatur: ✠John M. D'Arcy, D.D., M.A., S.T.D.
       Bishop of Fort Wayne-South Bend
       November 24,1986

ISBN 0-87973-072-2

Published, printed, and bound in the United States of America by
Our Sunday Visitor Publishing Division
Our Sunday Visitor, Inc.
200 Noll Plaza
Huntington, IN 46750

072

ACKNOWLEDGMENTS

Scripture texts used in this work are taken from the *New American Bible*, © 1970 by the Confraternity of Christian Doctrine, Washington, D.C., and are used by permission. All rights reserved.

Cover design: Rebecca J. O'Brien
Story illustrations: James McIlrath
Book design, activity art, and mechanicals: Rebecca J. O'Brien
Photos: Carol Fleming, O.P., Rev. Patrick McSherry, O.F.M. Cap., Rev. Lawrence Boadt, C.S.P., William Odell, Charles Savitskas, and John Zierten

The author and publisher acknowledge with thanks:
   McDonald's Corporation for permission to use the McDonald's name in the story line of Chapter 2.
   The Augustinians for permission to use the logo of the Sixteenth Centenary of the Conversion of St. Augustine in Chapter 1.
   Dan Paulos for permission to use his scissor cutting of the Assumption of Our Lady in Chapter 3.
   The Josephite Patoral Center, Washington, D.C. for permission to use the illustration of St. Martin de Porres in Chapter 4.
   The Sisters of St. Joan of Arc, Quebec for the depictions provided of St. Joan of Arc in Chapter 5.

Contents

Mike Miller

Mark Klopenstine

Susan Dewey

Mike Murphy

Mike Lewis

Kristie Marks

Brian Griman

Shelley L. Valenti

Sean Stump

Lisa Bodey

David Reinke

Rikki Bober

The class that piloted 'Empowered by the Spirit.' Back row, left to right: Michael Miller, Mark Klopenstine, Susan Dewey, Michael Murphy, Michael Lewis, Brian Griman, Kristie Marks, Shelley Valenti. Front row: David Reinke, Lisa Bodey, Sean Stump, Rikki Bober.

Photo by William E. Odell

Welcome to Empowered by the Spirit. We were the first students to use this book and become acquainted with Mark, Melissa, Jesse, Juanita, and their "heaven sent" teacher, Augustine. We hope you enjoy the stories and learn their messages as much as we did. May God bless you as you prepare to receive the Sacrament of Confirmation.

Chapter 1

You Will Receive Power

The Story Begins

At school, thought 14-year-old Mark McIntyre, everyone had seemed grumpy all day. Maybe it was the gray, gloomy day. He leaned against the school building and watched busses pull out of the lot. Then Mark laid his books down and pulled a hat over his dark, curly hair. With the hair and blue eyes, friends said, he looked just like Melissa, his twin sister.

But Melissa was the twin often in trouble. She was still in school, staying late at detention for talking in class. Mark was irritated because their parents insisted that they come home together. Mark spotted Jesse Hamilton and Juanita Sanchez walking toward him. They were good friends who rode the bus with the twins.

"We decided to walk home with you and Melissa," Jesse yelled from the middle of the lot.

Just then, the school doors flew open. Melissa burst into "freedom," her blue eyes flashing with an-

ger. Mark avoided any comment about her detention. The four headed up Maple Street to make the mile-long walk home.

"Hey guys, let's go check out the old Bentley house on Oak Street," Jesse suggested. "I've heard that the place is haunted," he said, flexing muscles to show that they'd be in no danger.

"Sure, Jesse, and you've got spooks in the brain," snapped Melissa, tossing her dark hair.

"Well, I've heard creepy things about that house too, Melissa," said Juanita. She was slim, dark-haired, pretty, and very cautious.

"If it gives Juanita the creeps, then it'll be fun to do," Jesse laughed, nudging Mark.

"Yeah, let's go," Mark added, getting enthused. "We need something to spice up the day."

The old Bentley house looked even gloomier under the cloudy afternoon skies. White paint was peeling to the bare wood, and the green shutters were hanging at crazy angles. There wasn't a window that hadn't been broken, and the porch was sagging.

At Jesse's suggestion, they sneaked around to the back to try to get in. They kicked aside old cans and picked their way through broken bottles and overgrown weeds. Mark and Jesse pulled off boards nailed over the back door. The lock had been broken. The door pushed open. The place was dark, full of dust and cobwebs as the four walked through the grand old downstairs rooms. But then they headed up the creaky steps to inspect the upstairs.

"Look, there's still some old furniture here," Mark said, looking into the master bedroom. Suddenly they heard footsteps downstairs in the front hallway.

The Strange Encounter

"Now we're in for it," Melissa whispered. "Whose idea was this, anyway?"

They tiptoed over to the top of the stairs to see if they could make a quick escape. But at the bottom of the stairs was a tall, elderly man with glasses. He looked back at them as though he wasn't at all surprised to see them.

"Come on down. I won't hurt you," called the man. He looked harmless. The voice seemed kind, with just the trace of an accent. Jesse started down, and the others followed.

"We weren't doing anything, Mister," Mark called down. "Really, we were just looking around. We heard the place was haunted."

"Well, in a way, I guess there is a spirit here," the man smiled. He was tanned, had jet-black eyes, and a white shock of hair. He was dressed in a zip-up lightweight jacket and corduroy slacks. He looked casual, yet somehow crisp and dignified. And there was also something foreign about the accent, something distant about him.

"What are your names?" he asked, folding his arms, kicking at an old bottle on the floor.

After the introductions, the four felt more relaxed. Even if they had come into a house with a "Keep Out" sign on it, this man didn't seem upset.

"Do you own this place?" Mark asked.

"No," the man replied softly, "but I think I have a good reason for being here."

"What's your name?" inquired Melissa boldly.

The man dusted some cobwebs off his sleeve, squared his shoulders, and suddenly looked very formal. *"Nomen meum est Aurelius Augustinus,"* he said with great dignity.

"Say what?" exclaimed Melissa.

"In your own tongue," replied the man, smiling, "my name is *Aurelius Augustinus.*"

"Yeah and my brother's Arnold Schwarzenegger," Melissa shot back.

Mark, Jesse, and Juanita glared at her, but the man with the big name didn't seem to mind.

"If that sounds too fancy," the man said, staring at Melissa, "you could call me Augustine. Most people of your nation have called me that."

"Are you famous or something?" Mark asked, studying the man's face.

"Well," said Augustine, "that's a good question, but the answer will take a while. Have you youngsters got a little time?"

The warm, open smile, the mysterious look somehow drew them like a magnet. Jesse and Mark found wooden crates to sit on. The four sat in the hallway to hear the strange, dignified man, who unzipped his jacket and sat down on one of the stairsteps.

Augustine Tells His Story

"You see," began Augustine, rubbing his hands together, "I'm a little bit like this old house. You see this house here and now, but really, it is part of the past. This will be hard for you to understand," he said, drawing a deep breath, "but I am from the very distant past."

"Just how old are you?" demanded Mark, not sure he fully understood what he had just heard.

"Over sixteen hundred years old," answered Augustine, without blinking an eye.

Melissa began to giggle. Jesse shot up off his stool and knocked it over. "Let's get out of here. This guy's daffy," he barked at Mark.

"No one lives sixteen hundred years!" Mark scoffed.

"I didn't say I'd lived that long. I gave you my age," Augustine answered. "You are certainly free to believe whatever you want. It is hard to believe that I am older than Abraham Lincoln or Christopher Columbus or Francis of Assisi, but I most certainly am."

Melissa's mouth dropped open. Juanita and Jesse simply backed away. Only Mark stayed put. Augustine rose from the stairs and walked toward him.

"Some people have a hard time believing in anything," Augustine said, looking down into Mark's face. Mark felt something like lightning go through his body. He nodded vaguely at Augustine's remark.

'Jesse shot up off his stool and knocked it over.'

"I don't know anybody better than a sixteen-hundred-year-old Father of the Church to prepare you four for Confirmation. After all, I've had so long to prepare," Augustine said.

"How did you know about our Confirmation?" gasped Melissa. "We just met you."

"Heaven's hotline told me," Augustine said. "But, as always, you have to be willing to believe in heaven's help." Clearly, there was now a tone of hurt in the old man's voice. Augustine zipped up his jacket and moved toward the door.

"Wait!" yelled Mark, sensing the loss of a great opportunity if Augustine walked out the door. Augustine turned around.

"Suppose," Mark suggested, "that we agree to be-lieve in you . . . at least for now. Will you stick around? I'd like to hear what you have to say."

"Yeah," Melissa interrupted, "if you're a fraud, we'll find out."

The look of injured pride swept over Augustine's face, but his hand dropped away from the doorknob. "You two," he said, "have a lot to learn about faith. But let's go over there and get started."

Mark, Melissa, Jesse, and Juanita trooped after the tall, white-haired Augustine into the next room, the Bentleys' old living room. There was still some old furniture there. Augustine sat down carefully in one of the sturdier chairs.

"I must tell you a story about preparing for what God sends to you," he said. "It's a story that you must understand. Soon you will be receiving something very great." His voice shook just a bit at the word *great*.

Pentecost Needs Preparation

"Do you remember the story of Pentecost?" Augustine asked. His chair groaned, and he made a face that made even Melissa laugh.

"Sure. That's when the tongues of fire came down on the Apostles," Juanita answered.

"That's right," Augustine said. "But to understand Pentecost, let's step back a bit in time.

"Do you recall times when you were confused because of all the choices facing you?" Augustine asked. "Or, have you ever felt nervous because you didn't know what to do? You looked for someone who would understand or offer help." The four thought for a moment, but Mark spoke first.

"My dad was laid off just before Christmas last year," he said. "I was hoping to get a certain Christmas gift, but I knew there was no chance for it then. I felt sorry for myself, but I could see that I was thinking only of myself. Later I started to worry about how Dad felt. Something helped me to see that Christmas was more than 'gimme, gimme.'"

"I was scared when my dad divorced Mom," Juanita said quietly. "I felt alone, and my mother was so upset. I wanted to help her, but she had always been the one to help me. My dad was upset too. I was angry and wanted things to be as they were. I've begun to see that I still love them both and that they need love from me. But sometimes I'm still confused."

"Okay," Augustine said. "You two had to make choices about how to handle something difficult. But you both grew from these things, and a change inside helped you.

"The best friends of Jesus, the Apostles, had an experience like yours," Augustine said. His story went like this.

Preparation for the First Pentecost

It was Passover time in Jerusalem in a year that we now call A.D. 33. For nearly three years, the Twelve Apostles had followed Jesus everywhere. Just a few days earlier, he had entered Jerusalem in triumph. Now he was on trial. They still didn't understand what was happening to his kingdom or why he was being mistreated. The "trial" he received was a farce, and the Apostles were powerless with fear. He suffered a beating by Roman soldiers, but rejection by his people hurt him more. He was God's Son, who had come to save them.

On the day after he was arrested, Jesus was crucified and died. For the Apostles, losing Jesus was

even more than losing a mother, father, sister, brother, grandparent, and best friend all at the same time. Today, those of us who have lost a loved one have some idea of how they felt. These grown men were just sick with anguish. And because they were so confused and afraid, they disappeared into hiding in a secret room in Jerusalem.

Then, on the third day after Jesus' death, news came that he had risen from the dead. While the Apostles were still in hiding, Jesus appeared to them and to his mother, who was also with them. At first, they thought that he was a ghost. But when they realized that he was truly the risen Lord, they were overcome with joy and wonder. He reminded them that the Scriptures had to be fulfilled by his suffering, death, and resurrection.

Jesus gave them a very important instruction. He told them to remain in the city until they were "clothed with power from on high."[1] Then, he reminded them that John had baptized them with water, but that they would be baptized with the Holy Spirit. "You will receive power when the Holy Spirit comes down on you."[2]

Power they did receive —

a powerful gift of grace. They were all together one day when a terrific wind was heard outside, and tongues of fire came upon them. Fear left them, and they began to speak about Jesus with boldness and joy. Everyone realized that a great change had taken place in them. With this great giving of the Spirit, their Confirmation, the Church began its public witness and spread throughout the world.

The Power Is for Everyone

"And you will receive power, too, when you are confirmed," Augustine said, finishing the story.

"Gee, maybe nobody will make me stay after school then," Melissa joked.

"I bet I know what this power is like," Jesse pitched in, with a look of triumph. "It's a kind of force, something that is with you and changes you."

"Well," Augustine replied, "there are some similarities. The Spirit is *with* you, and he gives you power. It is a power working through you to do the work of the Spirit, not your work. Remember, the Apostles spoke 'as the Spirit prompted them.'[3] That power is really a surge of God's love and strength in your souls, which is also known as grace."

"Just what is the Holy Spirit?" Juanita asked with a puzzled look.

"The question is *who* is the Holy Spirit?" Augustine said. "You know about the Trinity?"

"Father, Son, and Holy Spirit," Juanita answered.

"Yes, the Blessed Trinity is three *persons*," Augustine said. "The Father is really a person. And so is the Son and so is the Holy Spirit. And they are all one God. That is the faith of the Church. But every person has a personality and isn't just some abstract force. The Holy Spirit is a distinct person too. How would you describe your personalities?"

"Melissa is moody and too quick with the lip," Mark quickly responded.

"Well," Melissa bristled, "I think you're boring. I always know what you're going to do."

"Mark's right, Melissa," Jesse laughed. "You are moody, but Mark's shy, not boring."

It is a surge of God's love in your souls, called grace.

"How would you describe yourself, Jesse?" Augustine asked.

"See these fists?" Jesse smiled. "I'm a guy that won't take any nonsense."

"When he looks stern, he looks mean," Juanita added, "but underneath he has a heart as sweet and soft as cotton candy." Jesse blushed as the others laughed.

"Juanita is funny and very sensitive." Mark added.

"Well," said Augustine, "we'll discover more about ourselves soon. But one word describes the Holy Spirit to a *T*. 'Loving!' God's love pours into our hearts through the Holy Spirit."

Augustine looked out the dirty window and squinted. "I see that it's getting late," he said. "You must get home, but I'll see you soon."

In the hallway, the man who claimed sixteen hundred years put his shoulder against the front door which had been nailed shut from the outside. The sound of wood splintering around the door frame shocked the four. Augustine pushed the door open and stood in the doorway.

"See ya," said a wide-eyed Jesse with new respect for this white-haired man.

"May the Spirit be with you all," Augustine said with mock flourish.

Mark, Melissa, Jesse, and Juanita walked out the front door and headed toward their homes. "Who'd ever believe the things that happened today, even if we told them?" asked Melissa. Jesse started to say something, but then just nodded his head.

[1] Luke 24.49.
[2] Acts 1.8.
[3] *Ibid.*, 2.4.

St. Augustine

When *Aurelius Augustinus* was born in Africa in 354, his mother, Monica, knew that he might have a hard time finding the right road to God. Monica was a very faithful Catholic Christian who later became a saint. But Patricius, the baby's father, was a follower of the official religion, which worshiped many different gods and goddesses. Patricius was also an official of the Roman Empire in this Province of Numidia, which is now called Algeria.

Augustinus, or Augustine, was a very bright child, and his father tried to give him the best education available. At seventeen, the young man was sent off to the nearby city of Carthage for more schooling. Free from his parents' supervision, Augustine began to concentrate more on having a good time than on studying. He had a love affair with a young woman who gave birth to his son, *Adeodatus*, a name that in Latin means "gift of God."

But Augustine also began to stray from the proper path in other ways. He became "brainwashed" by a sort of cult religion called Manichaeism. It believed that all physical things, including human bodies, were evil. Manichaeans, therefore, thought that marriage and having children were wrong. Augustine, in his youthful innocence and perhaps from guilt, accepted this belief.

When Monica discovered how Augustine was living, she was heartbroken. She had taught her son Christian values, but he was rejecting them all. With the faith that Augustine laughed at, his mother began to pray almost constantly for his conversion. Some of her prayers had already been answered. Not long after Augustine left home, his father died. The man who had scorned belief in Christ received the gift of faith and became a Catholic on his deathbed.

Logo used by permission of the Augustinians

The logo for the Sixteenth Centenary of Saint Augustine's conversion shows Augustine with the two most important persons in his life, Monica and Ambrose.

In 383, at age twenty-nine, Augustine decided to go to Rome to continue his career of teaching. But he wasn't happy and went to teach at Milan, Italy the next year. With Adeodatus, Monica followed her son and continued to pray for him. It was in Milan that Augustine's life began to move in a new direction. Always impressed by intellectual brilliance, Augustine was slowly moved by the faith and wisdom of the most famous Catholic teacher of the day, Ambrose, bishop of Milan.

The influence of Ambrose and the

Photo by John Zierten

Augustine's life and message still intrigue the searching mind.

prayers of Monica were rewarded. At age thirty-two, right before Easter in 387, Augustine was baptized. Years later, he wrote about his early life and conversion in a book called *Confessions.*

With a new faith, Augustine believed that God wanted him to return to Africa. But he didn't know what he was to do there. Augustine had a vision that helped him see the work he was to begin. On the way back to Africa, Augustine and his mother were delayed in Ostia, where Monica fell ill and died. Soon after, Adeodatus died. These were terrible losses for Augustine, but his new faith began to fill his life. He began to teach about Christianity with great power.

Four years later, in 391, he was asked to become a priest, and he agreed to do so. Monica would have loved to see that day. In 395, just four years later and only eight years after his conversion, Augustine was made the Bishop of Hippo in Africa.

Augustine's teaching and example were especially needed in this age. The Roman Empire was beginning to collapse, and many false ideas were challenging the true Faith. As the empire was falling apart, Augustine taught about a new world that would one day take its place. He wrote about it in one of his most famous books, *The City of God.*

Augustine said that in discovering God, we discover ourselves. He had good reason to know what he was talking about. For the Faith he had come to love, he left over 100 books and many other writings. But perhaps his greatest gift was his powerful example of turning toward God.

13

Who Is the Holy Spirit?

Find the following verses from Scripture and write down what they tell us about the Holy Spirit.

Acts 11.12 _____ .

Romans 8.26 _____ .

Ephesians 4.30 _____ .

1 Corinthians 12.7 _____ .

Acts 20.23 _____ .

2 Corinthians 3.6 _____ .

Ephesians 4.3 _____ .

Romans 15.13 _____ .

1 Timothy 4.1 _____ .

Acts 15.28 _____ .

2 Corinthians 3.17 _____ .

Romans 14.17 _____ .

1 Corinthians 2.4 _____ .

Acts 13.4 _____ .

Compose a paragraph describing who the Holy Spirit is.

A Young Teen's Book of Catholic Knowledge

1. **What happened at Pentecost?**
   The Apostles were filled with the Holy Spirit.

2. **What did the Apostles receive when they received the Holy Spirit?**
   They received God's grace or power.

3. **How did the Apostles change after they received the Holy Spirit?**
   They proclaimed the Lord boldly; they spoke in foreign tongues.

4. **Do we receive the powerful grace of the Holy Spirit when we are confirmed?**
   Yes.

5. **What is different about the power we receive from the Holy Spirit?**
   It is the power, or grace, of the Holy Spirit working in us. He gives it to do his work, not ours. It comes to us as a gift, which we are to claim as our own.

6. **Is it more correct to say "What is the Holy Spirit?" or "Who is the Holy Spirit?"**
   Who is the Holy Spirit?

7. **How does the Church describe the Holy Spirit?**
   The Holy Spirit is the Third Person of the Blessed Trinity.

8. **Why is it important to know the Holy Spirit is a person?**
   Because he is a person, we are able to relate to the Spirit in a personal way. We can speak and pray to him, listen to him and work with him.

9. **What do we say about the Spirit in the Creed we say at Mass?**
   . . . the Holy Spirit, the Lord, the giver of life, who proceeds from the Father and the Son. . . . he is worshipped and glorified. He has spoken through the Prophets.

10. **What does it mean that the Spirit is holy?**
    He comes from the Father and the Son; he is the source of holiness to all who believe in him.

11. **What does it mean that the Spirit is the giver of life?**
    He is the source of life, the life of God, and eternal life.

12. **What is grace?**
    Grace is God's divine life, which is given to us as a gift. It is given to us in different ways. The sacraments are very special ways of receiving grace. Grace is a relationship with God lived by faith. It has the power to assist us to live with hope and genuine love.

Chapter 2

You Will Be My Witnesses

An Incident at Memorial Park

Mark, Melissa, Jesse, and Juanita had decided not to say anything to anyone about the encounter with Augustine at the Bentley house. "Could he really be who he says he is?" Jesse had wondered out loud. The other three had no answers. They were only beginning to give their beliefs some serious thought.

On the following Saturday, the sun was shining brightly. In the morning, Mark and Melissa hustled to do their own chores. Their dad had given them some theater passes. The twins were meeting Jesse and Juanita for lunch at McDonald's. From there, it was off to the movies.

McDonald's was about a fifteen-minute walk from the McIntyres'. Crisscrossing through Memorial Park, Mark and Melissa approached the playground area a little after twelve noon. Suddenly, they heard a child screaming.

As Mark ran around the big fir trees that had blocked his view, he could see what was happening. Five ninth

graders he knew had taken a Frisbee away from four small boys. Mark watched as Rick Johnson pushed one little boy away from the Frisbee on the ground and laughingly pitched it to Greg Schwartz. The little boy slumped to the ground in tears.

"Hey, McIntyre, come on and join the fun," yelled Rick.

The twins could see that the five older boys were having a good time. "It's not our business," Mark mumbled to Melissa.

"Right," she agreed, "and I don't want to be late. Juanita and Jesse are probably already waiting for us."

Without another word, they jogged away. But Mark soon began to break into an open field run. He soon left Melissa far behind. At the edge of the park, he started to run backwards, teasing Melissa to hurry up. And then . . . .

"Oooow," Mark yelled as he banged into something hard. It knocked him face down to the ground. As he rolled over and shook his head, he saw that he'd run into a group of older men pitching horseshoes. A large white-haired man sprawled next to him.

"It's you!" gasped Mark, looking straight into the face of Augustine. "Did I hurt you?"

"Oh, you know that you can't kill me!" laughed Augustine rubbing his head. One hand was still clutching a horseshoe. Mark jumped to his feet to help the other men with Augustine. Just then, Melissa caught up.

"Er . . . Mr. Augustine!" Melissa exclaimed. "What are you doing here?"

"Well," the older man answered, "I was just about to win this game of horseshoes. But now I think it's time to quit. Thanks, Jack. Thanks, Pete," he smiled, clapping one man on the shoulder. Dusting off some dead leaves from his pants legs, Augustine then straightened out the heavy white fisherman's sweater he was wearing. "Going my

way?" he asked, nodding toward the famous McDonald's arches down the block.

"Well, yes," answered Mark, looking up into Augustine's brown eyes. "We're meeting Juanita and Jesse at McDonald's." He hesitated but then added, "But why don't you let the McIntyres buy your lunch? Least we can do after I knocked you down. Uhh . . . do you eat Big Macs?"

In another moment, Augustine was strolling across the street with a twin on each side. He was willing to "try" one Big Mac, he told them. Inside, Mark went to the counter to place their orders, including a double order of fries for his sister. Melissa and Augustine headed toward a booth where Jesse and Juanita were already seated with their food. They greeted the mysterious Mr. Augustine with surprise. After he sat down, Augustine began to study the place as though he'd never seen anything like it.

As Augustine finished his burger a little later, he looked over at Melissa and Mark with gratitude. "This Big Mac is as good as any dish I've ever had — even in Rome! Thank you!" he said wiping his mouth with a napkin. But the twins noticed that his fries had gone untouched.

"You're welcome," said Mark with pride. "I'm glad we ran into you. I mean . . ."

It was too late! The man who claimed to be a saint and Doctor of the Church was roaring with laughter at Mark's unintended pun. Finally, Augustine recovered and ran his long, thin hand through his white hair.

After they were all finished, Augustine went back up to the counter to order a cup of tea. But he returned to the table with a chocolate shake instead. They didn't have his brand of tea, he explained. "And this looked so tasty!"

Do It for the Lord

"Can we talk for just a few more moments?" Augustine asked, slurping away at his shake. "Then, I know you must be off to the movies," he added.

"Sure," answered Jesse, "we've got time." Something in the strange old man drew them all. They didn't mind being with him or listening to him.

"Probably all four of you can think of something that you worked hard to accomplish," began Augustine between drags on the straw.

"Maybe you really gave it your best and later saw that it turned out better than you expected."

"Yeah," Jesse piped up. "I remember when we beat the undefeated football team. We were nervous when we went out on the field. But we won . . . and what a feeling!"

'Our friends will think we've gone weird.'

"Last Thanksgiving, I worked in the Thanks for Life drive," Juanita added. "When it was done, we had more food and clothing than anyone expected. It was so good to see the happy faces when people came to pick up the gifts."

"I had trouble in math last year," Mark pitched in. "I had to work awfully hard and wasn't sure I would pass. When I got my final exam back, not only did I pass, but I got an 'A'!"

"Good!" Augustine exclaimed. "You know, I have seen more people glow with that sort of joy than you could count. But one of the best stories is about the Apostles." Then, Augustine stopped talking for a mo-

ment to finish the shake he was apparently enjoying. He made a slurping noise with the straw, which seemed to surprise him. Augustine could see that a woman in a nearby booth was looking at him rather strangely. He nodded to her with a smile but continued.

"I didn't know the Apostles," Augustine joked, winking at Juanita. "They were a few hundred years before my time."

"Oh, really!" gasped Melissa dramatically. Mark and the other two laughed, and so did Augustine.

"Do you remember," Augustine asked, "how nervous the Apostles were just before they received the Holy Spirit?" His listeners nodded. "When it happened, they were amazed. Things turned out so much better than they had expected. Do you know what followed?"

"More or less," Mark answered, but the puzzled looks led Augustine to continue.

"Well, they left the place where they had been hiding and went out among the people there in Jerusalem. They took a great risk in doing that because they could have been arrested. They simply started to tell the people about Jesus Christ. They were so overwhelmed with the joy and power of the Holy Spirit that they were accused of being drunk."

Jesse chuckled at that thought.

"You wouldn't be missing the point, Jesse, would you?" Augustine chuckled in response.

"The Apostle Peter," Augustine continued, "concluded his speech by telling the crowd that the Jesus they crucified was made both Lord and Messiah by God. The people were stunned by the power of his words. When the people asked what they should do, Peter said that Jesus would save any person who would reform and be baptized in his name. By letting the Spirit speak through them and openly proclaiming Jesus as Lord of life, the Apostles had become real witnesses."

"That was fine for the Apostles," Melissa said. "Is that what we're supposed to do after we get confirmed? Our friends will think we've gone weird."

"Well," laughed Augustine, "you might not do it the same way."

"Then, how do we become witnesses?" Juanita asked.

"The Apostles were strengthened in the Holy Spirit at Pentecost. You will be too when you are confirmed. You too will need to listen to the promptings of the Holy Spirit in your lives by following your conscience and by doing good for others," Augustine continued. "In the case of the Apostles, they spoke as the Spirit prompted them — not just for their day and time, but for all times. The Spirit was in them, and they let the Spirit speak through them. In your case, however, the Spirit will have different tasks of discipleship and witness. Yet, you still need to release him, to let him speak and act through you as he chooses. That's what the Apostles did.

'You should have busted them in the chops,' Jesse said.

"The effect of this Pentecost was so wonderful in Jerusalem," Augustine said with great feeling. "Other things started to happen after the Holy Spirit was released. People were deeply affected by the change they saw in the Apostles. A Christian community began to grow. About three thousand people were baptized on the day of Pentecost.

That was really the beginning of the Church. Every day, new people became converts to the community. They worshiped together, prayed together, and shared in common needs."

Put on the Lord Jesus Christ

"Do you remember what a convert is?" asked Augustine suddenly.

"I always thought it was someone who joined the Catholic Church?" Mark answered.

"The word has been used that way," Augustine said, looking at Mark. "There are two meanings for all Christians today. First, a convert is someone who has repented of past sin, or turned away from everything that is against Christ. Second, the word describes someone who has accepted Jesus Christ as the Lord of his or her life."

"You were a convert, weren't you?" offered Juanita. Augustine smiled in approval. "Tell us how it happened," Juanita pleaded.

"Okay," Augustine agreed, "I'll give you a short version now, or you'll miss your movie."

As he began, he looked very far away. "Remember when I told you about myself last time, how I lived a reckless life as a teenager. I let my passions get the better of me and was involved in sinful relationships. Well, the pain of my life caught up with me. I tried to change, but I would easily fall back into old, bad habits. It was a kind of bondage with really no happiness in it. I did not like what I saw in myself. I also knew there was a life after death and a judgment to come. I was approaching my conversion. When it finally happened, I broke down and ran to a secluded part of the garden. Underneath a fig tree, I fell to my face sobbing and praying.

"All of a sudden, I heard the voice of a child coming from a neighbor's house. The voice said, 'Take it, read it! Take it, read it!' I got up and simply opened my scroll — we didn't have books back then — to just anyplace. My eye caught the following passage from Romans: 'Let us live honorably as in daylight; not in carousing and drunkenness, not in sexual excess and lust, not in quarreling and jealousy. Rather, put on the Lord Jesus Christ and make no provision for the desires of the flesh.'[1] Very silently, a peace and calm came over me."

Even Melissa was stunned

by his story. They stared at one another with wide-eyed wonder. His story even caught the attention of some people at nearby tables. Augustine gave them all a big grin. Then he shifted in his seat and cleared his throat to continue.

"There were many converts before me and many since. One of the most famous conversions is described in the Acts of the Apostles shortly after the Pentecost story. That was the story of the conversion of Paul. He was a changed man.

"I remember something about his being thrown to the ground," Juanita said.

"He did get quite a jolt," Augustine agreed.

"Do you know what happened after Paul's conversion?'' Augustine asked.

"He stopped picking on the Christians,'' Melissa said bluntly.

"Yes, that is what he stopped doing,'' Augustine said. "He reformed his life. He asked for forgiveness for the wrongs he had done. But he also made some positive changes. He was baptized as you were and made promises as your parents made for you. In the Sacrament of Confirmation, you will be able to renew those promises, to say for yourself that you will live in the Lord.''

"Didn't Paul begin to do a lot of traveling then?'' asked Jesse.

"Yes,'' Augustine said. "He became as active in speaking for Jesus as he had once been in speaking against him. His actions were a strong witness to the Lord. Paul became his Apostle.''

Playground Incident Revisited

"Okay,'' interrupted Melissa, "but Paul was a grown man. At our age, we can't really speak for Jesus or witness like that. And we'd be hooted out of school if we went around that way.''

"Is that what you were afraid of at the playground today?'' Augustine asked.

Mark suddenly started to cough, and Melissa looked very uncomfortable. With a few words, Melissa shyly told Jesse and Juanita about how she and Mark had ignored the bullying of some small boys by ninth graders they knew.

You could have made them forget their hurt.

"I'm not trying to judge you two,'' said Augustine. He offered his untouched french fries to Melissa as a peace offering. "I'm trying to show you something about discipleship and the need for conversion. Even though you didn't join the bullies, you felt guilty about not speaking out, didn't you?''

"Yeah,'' Mark said softly.

"You should have busted them in the chops,'' Jesse said, throwing a make-believe punch.

"I guess we should have told them to leave the little kids alone, too,'' Melissa added. "They might have made fun of us but. . . .''

Juanita had been deep in thought. "Maybe,'' she broke in, "it would have been good to take some time to play with the kids, to make them forget their hurt.''

"Yes. Juanita has made my point for me,'' Augustine responded. "Telling the bullies to stop would have been an attempt to stop a wrong. That's good. But caring for the hurt children by giving them some attention would have been a real witness. That's doing it the way Jesus would have done.''

Mark asked, "You mean we really can be disciples of Jesus *now?*''

"Yes, yes,'' Augustine replied, suddenly stuffing some of Melissa's fries into his mouth. "All of you can be disciples now. But speaking of now, I think it's time for you to go.'' He stood up suddenly, startling the lady who'd been staring at him earlier. Augustine grinned a silly grin for her.

"You have plenty of time to get to your double feature if you hurry,'' Augustine said once they were gathered outside. "See you soon.''

"Hey, how did you know we were going to a double feature?'' Melissa demanded.

But Augustine only laughed. He headed down the street walking like a young man!

¹ Romans 13.13-14.

St. Paul

Grinding his teeth in anger, a man shouted, "Kill him! Let the blasphemer be stoned to death!" Those could have been the words of a man named Saul to the deacon Stephen, the first of the Christian martyrs. Saul was there when Stephen was stoned to death, holding the cloaks of Stephen's executioners.

Cold stone captures a fiery St. Paul with his sword of God's Word.

Photo by Charles A. Savitskas

That doesn't seem like a very good beginning for one of Christ's most important disciples and a saint of the Church, does it? Why was Saul so full of hatred for the disciples of the Lord? Life had been good to him. He was born a citizen of the Roman Empire, which carried many privileges. He learned the trade of a tentmaker, which was a profitable trade to have at the time. He was also brought up as a strict Pharisee. He was devoted to his practice of the Jewish faith but was also suspicious of anything that opposed the strict practices he had accepted. This new faith of the disciples of Jesus was most threatening, and he reacted typically for a hot-blooded, strong-minded man.

His murderous threats didn't stop with the stoning of Stephen. Saul enthusiastically joined in making it hard on the new Church. He and others entered house after house, dragging men and women out, and throwing them into jail (Acts 8.3). When many moved away to avoid his persecution, he extended his search even to Damascus.

On the road to Damascus, Saul's life changed. A light from the sky flashed about him. He fell to the ground and heard a voice asking, "Saul, Saul, why do you persecute me?" It was the voice of Jesus. Saul rose from the ground, blind. He was led on to Damascus by his

Photo by Rev. Lawrence Boadt, C.S.P.

Statues, arches, fountains, and other trappings of wealth lined this street in the city of Ephesus where St. Paul once walked and taught the people to turn away from false gods.

companions, and there the Lord sent Ananias to baptize Saul. Saul's sight was restored.

Did Saul immediately run out preaching Christ? No, he prepared to be a disciple. He spent much time learning about the mysteries of his new faith. He even spent long months in the desert, as Jesus had done, meditating and praying. When he did begin to speak publicly, neither the Christians nor the Jews trusted him. At first, the Christians couldn't believe he had truly become a disciple. The Jews, on the other hand, saw him as a traitor. In fact, some Jews tried to kill Saul in Damascus. He escaped by being lowered over a city wall in a basket.

About this time, Saul became better known by his Gentile name, Paul. He began to preach Christ with even more enthusiasm than he used to persecute Christ. It was Paul who was chosen by Jesus to spread the faith to non-Jewish people, the Gentiles. He went to them in Palestine and the surrounding nations. He became a tireless and powerful witness of the Lord and his saving message.

Was it easy being a disciple for the Lord? Listen to Paul's own words. "Five times at the hands of the Jews I received forty lashes less one; three times I was beaten with rods; I was stoned once, shipwrecked three times . . . I traveled continually, endangered by floods, robbers, my own people, the Gentiles; imperiled in the city, in the desert, at sea, by false brothers; enduring labor, hardship, many sleepless nights; in hunger and thirst and frequent fastings; in cold and nakedness" (2 Corinthians 11.24-27).

Why did he put up with all of that? Because his life truly changed. He said, ". . . the life I live now is not my own; Christ is living in me" (Galatians 2.20). He never lost heart because his inner self was fed every day by the Holy Spirit. For all the weariness his mind and body experienced, his inner self was full of joy, peace, and hope.

Something to Think About

"I was baptized and go to church, so conversion doesn't apply to me."
Is this statement TRUE or FALSE ? Think it through.

1. With _____ , I began the process of conversion.

   • I was _____ spiritually and made part of the Body of

   Christ, the Church.

   • I was cleansed of _____ _____ .

2. In the Sacrament of Confirmation, the Holy Spirit will be

_____ in me.

   • My responsibility increases to _____ live out

   the promises my parents first made for me in Baptism.

3. The Sacrament of the Eucharist feeds me with Christ's _____ and _____ , so that I regularly receive the nourishment I need to live the Christian life.

4. But sometimes I fail in keeping the faith promises I've made. I sometimes choose the way of _____ . Sin _____ me from Jesus and from his Body, the Church.

5. Because of sin, and temptation to sin, I am constantly in need of _____ , or turning away from sin.

6. So conversion is a life-long _____ . It doesn't end with Confirmation or with any particular event in life. I need constantly to make a new effort to turn my _____ and _____ over to Jesus Christ.

7. I am called to greater faith, repentance, and conversion _____ _____ of my life.

8. The sacrament that helps Catholics in their constant conversion is the Sacrament of _____ .

Steps to Discipleship

Find the following passages in Scripture and read what Jesus has to say about becoming a disciple. What effect do you think each could have in your life?

Matthew 16.24-26 _____

_____

_____

Matthew 10.24-25 _____

_____

_____

_____

Luke 9.59-62 _____

Luke 14.33 _____

_____

_____

Matthew 10.37 _____

_____

John 6.66-67 _____

_____

_____

_____

A Young Teen's Book of Catholic Knowledge

1. **What happens when you experience "conversion"?**
    - *Repentance* — turning away from sin and turning toward God. This is a gift of grace on God's part and a response to that grace on our part.
    - *Faith* — personal recognition of Jesus Christ as Lord and Savior, and the acceptance of the basic beliefs of the Church as stated in the Nicene Creed.
    - *Obedience* — personal acceptance of the authority of the Church's teaching in matters of faith and morality.
    - *Forgiveness* — having one's sins forgiven in the Sacrament of Reconciliation.

2. **Does conversion happen just once and then it is over with?**
    No. Although it can begin with a dramatic event, it is a process that takes a lifetime. Because of personal sin and human weakness, we are constantly in need of repentance, deeper faith, stronger conviction of belief, and obedience to the Church's rightful authority.

3. **What are sacraments?**
    Sacraments are special occasions when God gives us his very own life through Christ. Sacraments have signs and gestures that communicate how we are being touched by God's love. If we respond in faith, sacraments give us the grace to be true disciples of Christ.

4. **Which sacraments make us full members of Christ's Mystical Body, the Church?**
    Baptism, Confirmation, and the Eucharist. They are called sacraments of initiation.

5. **How does the Sacrament of Baptism begin the process of conversion?**
    Through the grace of the Holy Spirit, we are spiritually reborn, we are made members of Christ's Mystical Body, we become members of the Church, and we are cleansed of all sin.

6. **What is the sacrament that helps Catholics in converting from sin?**
    The Sacrament of Reconciliation, which a Catholic should celebrate regularly, is the ordinary way for a Catholic to get sins forgiven and is a powerful help in converting to God.

7. **How does the Sacrament of Confirmation lead us to discipleship?**
    We are strengthened by the Holy Spirit to be faithful followers and loyal witnesses of Christ.

8. **How does the Sacrament of the Eucharist strengthen discipes of Jesus?**
    In the Sacrament of the Eucharist, Christ becomes present to us in a very special way. When we receive this sacrament with open minds and hearts, we are nourished by Christ's Body and Blood, so that we can remain faithful.

Chapter 3

The Powerful Gift of Wonder and Awe

The Surprise Guest

The last chorus of "Holy God, We Praise Thy Name" was still playing at St. Patrick's noon Mass. Juanita, Jesse, Melissa, and Mark all found themselves at the tail end of the congregation leaving church. Mark and Melissa didn't usually attend this Mass, but this Sunday was Juanita's birthday. To celebrate, she had asked the other three to be her guests at the skating rink. Later, Juanita's mother was serving homemade Mexican food, cake, and ice cream.

Originally, Juanita had hoped to celebrate her birthday with a big pizza party the night before. But Sunday was the only day Mrs. Sanchez didn't have to work. And then Juanita realized that a pizza party for twenty or twenty-five kids was too expensive.

"Well, Happy Birthday, Juanita! I couldn't help overhearing . . ."

In the middle of a hug from Melissa, Juanita heard a man whose voice was now quite familiar. All four spotted Augustine standing right behind them as though he'd appeared out of nowhere. Dressed in a charcoal three-piece suit with a red tie, Augustine turned to Mrs. Sanchez, who was standing next to Juanita.

"You must be Mrs. Sanchez," Augustine said with a smile. "It's a pleasure to meet you."

"Thank you," answered a puzzled Clara Sanchez. "But I'm afraid I don't know you!"

"Mother, this is Mr. Augustine," intervened Juanita. "Uhh . . . we all met him several weeks ago. He's helping us with some extra studies for Confirmation."

"Oh, really?" commented Mrs. Sanchez. "Are you a teacher?"

"Well," said Augustine, catching Juanita's eye, "I once was. But I've been sort of retired for a long time. Seems like centuries!"

Mrs. Sanchez didn't understand why this last remark made Mark and Jesse choke with laughter, but her instincts told her that Mr. Augustine was really all

right. Suddenly, rain began to spot the pavement in front of St. Pat's.

"Oh, Mom!" Juanita moaned. "We'll get all wet walking to the skating rink!"

The four had planned to walk to the rink so that Juanita's mom could finish party preparations at home. There really wasn't time to take them and pick them up.

"Please, Mrs. Sanchez . . ." begged Augustine, "let me take them if there's a problem. I have my car and had nothing planned for the afternoon except to look over some dusty Latin manuscripts."

"That would help," agreed Juanita's mother, "but plan on staying later to have supper and cake."

Faces of Fear

Melissa, Jesse, and Juanita were soon squeezing into the back seat of Augustine's red car. Mark jumped into the front and agreed to give directions. The four noticed right away that Augustine was hardly an experienced driver. The red car jerked its way down the street to a stop sign. There, Mark showed Augustine a light lit on the dashboard. The parking brake was still on.

"Thank you," Augustine said, disgusted with himself. "I'm afraid of cars. But I wanted to talk to you about a different sort of fear," Augustine said, glancing at the three with his rearview mirror. "Will the birthday girl forgive me for bending your ear on her birthday?"

"Sure, Mr. Augustine," laughed Juanita.

"Well," Augustine began, "there is something that all of us older Christians once called *the gift of fear of the Lord*. What do you think fear of the Lord means?"

"I think it means we'd better not cross God," Melissa suggested half seriously.

"But isn't God supposed to be loving and forgiving?" Juanita countered.

"Yes," said Augustine. "He is, and 'fear of the Lord' is not like the fear I have of cars.

"That emotional type of fear can be both helpful and harmful," Augustine continued, jerking to a stop for a red light. "It's helpful when it protects us from doing something that is dangerous — such as taking drugs or alcohol."

"Or riding with Mr. Augustine?" his four passengers were wondering to themselves.

"But it is harmful when it pressures us to do something wrong or prevents us from doing something that is right."

"You mean like kids who drink," Mark asked, "because they're afraid of what their friends will think if they don't?"

"Yes, Mark." Augustine replied, and added, "Or when we just look the other way and don't say anything when we see a wrong being done."

God Is Number One!

"These days the Rite of Confirmation talks about a gift called *wonder and awe in the presence of the Lord.* It used to be called 'fear of the Lord,' " Augustine continued. "I think this new name is better. But God is providing a better way for me to describe this gift. Look at the rainbow."

"Oh, neat!" Melissa exclaimed. Stopped again at another light, all five were gazing up at the sky. The rainbow was just painting the sky with pinks, yellows, and blues. Honking from

several cars behind them reminded Augustine that the car wouldn't move unless he did. The red compact lurched around the corner and sped off.

"The way we reacted to the rainbow says something about what 'wonder and awe in the presence of the Lord' should mean," Augustine continued. "The Lord is so great, so loving, so merciful, so just that we should always have him in our minds and hearts. Once we really see him, we don't want to quit looking at him until we have to. And because the Lord is all those things, we should fear separation from him."

"I don't get it," Jesse piped up from the back seat.

"Think of what that rainbow added to our day," explained Augustine. "It added beauty and freshness. What do you think the world would be like if there were no smiling faces, no birthday parties, no beautiful trees or flowers, no autumn leaves, no snow for winter sports, or warm sunshine for summer games?"

"Yuk!" Melissa said with emphasis.

"I guess that sums it up, Melissa," Augustine laughed. "We want life to be full of those wonderful things. And because the Lord is so great, loving,

merciful, and just, we should never want to be separated from him.

"And because the Lord is all those things, he is number one," Augustine continued. Augustine's active gesturing while driving prompted Mark to reach around and fasten his seatbelt. "The Lord is so important to our life," insisted Augustine, "that we must honor him, make him number one. That is what the gift of 'wonder and awe in the presence of the Lord' helps us to do."

'I think it means we'd better not cross God.'

"The mother of Jesus understood this perfectly," Augustine continued, "even at your age. In her beautiful song, the 'Magnificat,' Mary prayed, 'His mercy is on those who fear him in every generation.' In other words, those who honor the Lord will be blessed by his mercy. Her whole life was spent honoring God. God, in her life, was number one.

"Do you also remember the story of Abraham and Isaac?" Augustine asked.

"Didn't God tell Abraham

to sacrifice Isaac?" Mark recalled.

"Yes," Augustine said, as they pulled into the skating-rink parking lot. But the four waited to hear the story once again. Augustine turned off the motor and swung around in his seat. His dark eyes were so bright that Melissa elbowed Juanita to draw her attention to them.

"Just as Abraham prepared his knife to sacrifice Isaac, a messenger from the Lord stopped him," Augustine said dramatically. "The angel said, 'Do not lay your hand on the boy . . . I know now how devoted you are to God, since you did not withhold from me your own beloved son.'[1] That's what it means to honor God. To be so devoted that nothing or no one comes before him!"

"Gee, I'm willing to sacrifice a certain family member," Melissa laughed, swinging open the car door. She hurried off with Juanita as Mark scowled at her. A moment later, Augustine strolled toward the roller rink with Mark and Jesse.

About an hour later, Juanita noted Augustine's look of relief when she told him it was time to head back home for the party. The music, he admitted, was a bit loud. And he couldn't see the point of rolling around and around in circles. Plus, he had become the center of attention for having sprawled on the floor a few too many times.

At the house, Mrs. Sanchez had transformed the dining room with purple crepe paper and pink balloons. Burritos, refried beans, soft drinks, and a large chocolate cake were all waiting, along with Juanita's grandmother and several aunts.

Seven Gifts and Lots of Power

After cake, Juanita happily attacked a small mountain of gifts. When she had finished, Augustine handed her a small, beautifully wrapped gift he took out of his coat pocket.

"Hey, Mr. Augustine," Jesse stared at him, "how could you have a gift for Juanita? You didn't know it was her birthday until after Mass? And then you were with us at the rink!"

But Augustine merely smiled that ancient smile. Inside the small box, Juanita found a beautiful little silver cross on a chain. Juanita's mother looked on in admiration.

"It looks old, Mr. Augustine," Mrs. Sanchez said, picking up the cross. "Is it antique?"

"Oh, it would be about as old as I am," he said, winking at a grateful Juanita.

In the living room, a little later, Mrs. Sanchez sat down with Juanita's grandmother and aunts who spoke only Spanish. Augustine settled into an easy chair. His four friends sat down cross-legged on the carpet to finish eating and to look at a game Juanita had received from Mark.

"Did you all notice Juanita's face as she opened the gifts?" Augustine asked.

"Yeah." Jesse volunteered. "Excited!"

"You know," Augustine continued, "Confirmation should be exciting too. Not only are you receiving the gift of the Spirit, but seven very special gifts of the Spirit as well."

"Great!" Melissa said. "What are they?"

"We talked about one of them earlier," Augustine said. "But before I tell you the other gifts of the Holy Spirit, let me ask you something about gifts. Melissa, what do you expect Juanita to do with that pretty sweater you gave her?"

"Wear it, of course," Melissa answered, giving Augustine a peculiar look.

"Seems like an obvious answer doesn't it?" Augustine said. "But what do you think the Holy Spirit expects you to do with the gifts you will receive from him?"

"Wear them?" Jesse joked.

"In a way," Augustine laughed. "In fact, St. Paul said we had to 'put on that new man'[2] when we are converted. In a sense, you do put on and wear those gifts. Melissa expects Juanita to use her gift; the Holy Spirit expects you to use the gifts he gives you in Confirmation."

"Okay," Mark said. "So just what are the gifts?"

"Well, they are gifts of power," Augustine began. "This power is a pouring in of God's love and strength that we know as grace. Remember that you will receive this power, or grace, when you receive the Sacrament of Confirmation. Remember, also, that it is the power of the Spirit in you. That power is contained in the gifts that the Spirit brings.

"So," as Augustine counted them on his fingers, "there's wisdom, understanding, knowledge, right judgment, courage, reverence, and finally, wonder and awe in the presence of the Lord."

Augustine was amused. Staring up at him from the living-room carpet were four of the blankest faces he'd ever seen in all his years! They didn't know what to make of these gifts.

"They sound . . . different," Mark said politely. "How'll we recognize them?"

"By what they will do for you," Augustine answered with enthusiasm, ". . . *if* you will open and use the gifts." Their faces were no longer blank but full of expectation.

"If you live by the Spirit," Augustine explained, "you will grow in the way he has planned for you."[3]

His rapt listeners looked at one another silently.

"Sounds nice," Jesse broke the silence, knowing his words didn't say enough.

Augustine laughed heartily. "Yes, very nice!"

"How about more cake?" interrupted Mrs. Sanchez. When she had filled four plates with second helpings of chocolate cake and ice cream, she sat down again with her mother.

"What about the gift of wonder and awe?" continued Mark. "How would we use that?"

Honor God and Give Him Glory

"The first thing," Augustine said, leaning back in his recliner, "would be to stop putting ourselves first — you know — thinking only of 'me, me, me'. There is that story in Luke's Gospel where Jesus is a guest at a meal in the house of a leading Pharisee. He noticed how many of the guests were trying to get the places of honor at the table. Jesus said that was wrong.

"The truth is that anyone who exalts himself puts God in a lesser place. There can be only one *number one* — God! So, we put the Lord first by truly making him Lord of our lives. And then, we don't let anything else become a god for us. And

we keep putting the Lord first by using his name respectfully in praise and thanksgiving and by never using his name loosely or hatefully."

"That sounds like one of the Commandments that God gave to Moses," Juanita said.

"Right," Augustine said. "It's the second which says: 'You shall not take the name of the LORD, your God, in vain.'[4] And not letting anything else be your god comes from the first: 'I, the LORD, am your God. You shall not have other gods besides me.'[5] Do you recall the third?"

"I think it's about not missing Mass," Melissa said, finishing off a bit of chocolate icing on her fork.

"Yes, it is," Augustine said. "It means that and more. It says: 'Remember to keep holy the sabbath day.'[6] It also asks us to use that day to take stock of our lives and see how we measure up to God's plan. The first three Commandments give us God's own guidelines for using this gift of wonder and awe.

"Listen," Augustine said, changing the mood a bit, "let's have a song. We'll ask your mother, grandmother, and aunts to join us. I'll teach you an old Christian song I learned when I first knew the Lord."

"That would be fun," said Juanita, "but *Abuela* (Grandmother) knows no English at all."

"No problem," he reassured her, "I'll teach it to you all in Spanish. Now let me see . . . ."

In a moment, Augustine had everyone gathered around Juanita's confused-looking Grandmother Alvarez on the sofa. He taught Jesse and Mark the melody round and set them singing — "God is love, and he is peace. Honor him and live in joy." Then came Juanita, Melissa, and one of Juanita's aunts. Finally, Abuela Alvarez and Juanita's mother and another aunt joined in. Abuela's old eyes laughed back at Augustine's.

As the last strains of the old musical round concluded, Augustine broke into "Happy Birthday." Juanita blushed deeply, as the warm baritone voice carried the song along loud enough for the neighbors to hear. Jesse and Mark laughed at Juanita's embarrassment, but her mother simply hugged her. It was, Juanita knew, a very good birthday.

[1] Genesis 22.12. [2] Ephesians 4.24.
[3] See 1 Corinthians 13.4-7; Galatians 5.22-23; Ephesians 5.9; 2 Corinthians 6.6; 2 Peter 1.5-7; and 1 Timothy 4.12 for St. Paul's various lists of the fruits of the Holy Spirit.
[4] [5] [6] See Exodus 20.1-8.

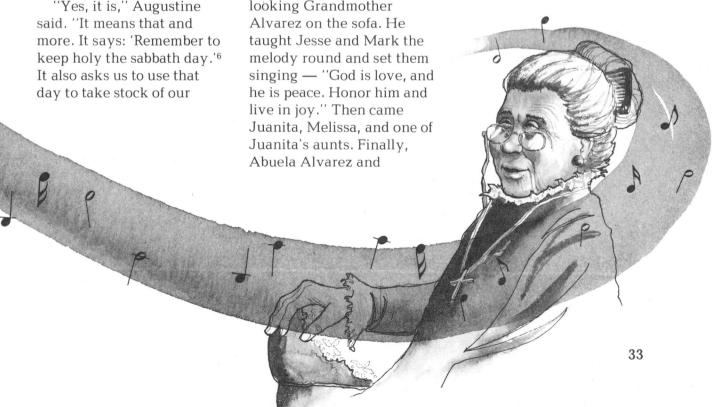

Mary, Jesus' Mother

"My being proclaims the greatness of the Lord, my spirit finds joy in God my savior" (Luke 1.46-47).

These words of praise, reverence, and awe poured out of a young girl who, according to the marriage customs of the time, was probably in her early teens. The scene was a special day almost two thousand years ago in a house in Palestine, a land now called Israel. The house belonged to an older

The Upper Room in Jerusalem where the Holy Spirit descended on Mary and the Apostles.

Photo by Holy Views Ltd.

At the end of her earthly life, Mary was taken into heaven body and soul.

couple, Zechariah and Elizabeth. Elizabeth was a cousin to Mary, or Miriam, the girl whose name was not unusual in Palestine.

If her name was common, the reason for Mary's overflowing joy was not! Mary had learned from the Angel Gabriel that she was to be the Virgin Mother of the Son of God, the promised Redeemer. The Church celebrates that moment as the Feast of the Annunciation. The Church also teaches that Mary was conceived without any stain of sin in her soul, since she was destined to become the sinless Mother of God. That is celebrated by the Church as the Feast of the Immaculate Conception.

When Mary returned home, she married Joseph, a carpenter, but remained a virgin. They had already been engaged. In due time, prophecies about the birth of the Savior were fulfilled. Mary gave birth to Jesus, the promised baby boy, in Bethlehem.

The Holy Family's life was quiet in Nazareth. Mary's tasks were typical for wives of the time. She had water to draw, bread to knead and bake, meals to prepare, and clothes of linen or wool to make or mend. Meals most likely consisted of homemade barley bread, beans cooked with oil or honey, onions, asparagus, tomatoes, and a wide range of fruits. Three times a day, the family prayed together, and three times a year, they traveled with others to celebrate feast days in Jerusalem.

Mary's influence on Jesus was especially evident at a wedding feast in Cana near Nazareth. She told Jesus that the wine had run out. Then, she said to the attendants, "Do whatever he tells you" (John 2.5). Ever since, her advice has been seen as a primary rule of

Christian discipleship: "Follow the commands of Jesus."

As Jesus traveled about Palestine, Mary sometimes followed. John's Gospel says that she was present at the Crucifixion. At the foot of the cross, Jesus gave his mother to his disciple John, but also to all of his followers. She became the Mother of the Church.

At Pentecost, Mary was waiting with the Apostles for the Holy Spirit her Son promised. And she was surely close at hand when Jesus ascended into heaven. The Church teaches that after the course of her earthly life, Mary was taken into heaven, body and soul. We celebrate that as the Feast of the Assumption. But, in a way, every day is a good day to celebrate and remember the wonderful faithfulness of Miriam, or Mary of Nazareth. She is the Mother of God, the Mother of the Church. And she was ever-faithful to God.

Who Is 'Our Father Who Art in Heaven'?

I. When do you feel closest to God?

On each blank space below, write the number that indicates how close to God you feel.

I feel close to God:

    1 — always   2 — often   3 — sometimes
    4 — rarely   5 — never

___ When I am with friends.

___ When I worship with other people at Sunday Mass.

___ When I am alone.

___ When I listen to music.

___ When I feel sad.

___ When I read the Bible.

___ When I have succeeded at something.

___ When I receive the Eucharist at Mass.

___ During a family activity.

___ When I pray in the Real Presence of the eucharistic Christ.

___ When I am helping someone.

___ When I feel helpless or confused.

___ When it is quiet.

___ When I feel happy.

___ When I'm close to nature.

___ In private prayer.

___ When I _____ _____

II. Attributes of God.

Write a paragraph describing what qualities or characteristics you would like God to have.

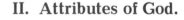

_____

_____

_____

III. Attributes of God According to Scripture.

Attributes of God are the words we use to describe God. Scripture tells about many of these attributes. They reflect the perfection of God.

First, look at the attributes of God that are reflected in the diamond. Then, one by one, look up the Scripture passages. In each box, as you read, write the number of the attribute that shines through the Scripture quote.

☐ Psalm 90.1-2

☐ 1 John 1.5

☐ Jeremiah 32.17

☐ Romans 10.12

☐ Psalm 139.7-10

☐ Psalm 19.2

☐ John 3.16

☐ Hebrews 4.13

☐ Romans 3.25-26

☐ Psalm 46.10

☐ 2 Timothy 2.11-13

☐ Malachi 3.6

6. All Knowing
2. All Powerful
10. Eternal
4. Glorious
3. Merciful
11. Just
5. Faithful
12. Holy
8. Love
7. Almighty
9. Everywhere
1. Constant

Which attribute of God is most important in your life now?

_____

Steps to Discipleship

Here are nine ways to honor God. Think about each of them and then record what you can do now to give honor to God.

1 "I, the LORD, am your God . . . . You shall not have other gods besides me" (Exodus 20.2-3).

I can _____

_____ .

2 "The heavens declare the glory of God, and the firmament proclaims his handiwork" (Psalm 19.2).

I can _____

_____ .

3 "Remember to keep holy the sabbath day" (Exodus 20.8).

I can _____

_____ .

4 "The LORD is my light and salvation; whom should I fear? (Psalm 27.1).

I can _____

_____ .

5 "His mother instructed those waiting on table, 'Do whatever he tells you' " (John 2.5).

I can _____

_____ .

6 "You shall not take the name of the LORD, your God, in vain" (Exodus 20.7).

I can _____

_____ .

7 "The LORD is my shepherd; I shall not want" (Psalm 23.1).

I can _____

_____ .

8 "God is light; in him there is no darkness" (1 John 1.5).

I can _____

_____ .

9 "All the paths of the LORD are kindness and constancy toward those who keep his covenant and his decrees" (Psalm 25.10).

I can _____

_____ .

A Young Teen's Book of Catholic Knowledge

1. **What are the seven gifts of the Holy Spirit?**
   Wisdom, understanding, knowledge, right judgment, courage, reverence, wonder and awe in the presence of the Lord.

2. **What do the seven gifts of the Holy Spirit help us to do?**
   They give us the power and grace that come from the Spirit, and strengthen us to be faithful witnesses to the Lord.

3. **What does the Holy Spirit expect us to do with his gifts?**
   To use these gifts to achieve greater personal holiness, in following the Commandments, and in doing good in our daily lives.

4. **What does the gift of "wonder and awe in the presence of the Lord" help us to do?**
   It strengthens us to honor the Lord.

5. **How do we honor God?**
   By knowing and loving him and by making him number one in our lives.

6. **What did Jesus' mother do to honor God?**
   She accepted God's invitation to be the mother of his Son, and she remained ever faithful to God.

7. **How did Abraham honor God?**
   He put God first in all things, even to the point of being willing to sacrifice his son, Isaac, if that was God's will.

8. **How can we honor God?**
   There are many ways, but the first three of the Ten Commandments teach us basic ways of honoring God.

9. **What does the First Commandment ask of us?**
   We are called to put God first in our lives and to not replace him with anyone or anything else.

10. **What is asked of us in the Second Commandment?**
    We should use God's name in praise and thanksgiving, and never abuse his name by using it loosely or hatefully.

11. **What does the Third Commandment say?**
    We should keep holy the Sabbath day, that is, honor each Sunday by worshiping God at Mass with our parish family and by giving time to family, to the service of others, and to other special activities.

12. **Should we feel afraid of God?**
    We should never feel afraid of God, because he wants only good for us. We should fear separation from God because he is so loving, merciful, and just.

Chapter 4

The Powerful Gift of Reverence

At the Car Wash

"I've had it with parents," Melissa growled to Sherri Simmons.

It seemed like a fine Saturday morning. Melissa and Mark McIntyre had been working with their classmates at the car wash near Memorial Park. In return for drying off and buffing cars as they came out of the wash, money was to be donated to St. Jude's, the city's hospital for handicapped children. But earlier in the morning, Melissa had had an argument with her mother. Mrs. McIntyre had grounded Melissa for two weeks following the car wash. Melissa couldn't get the matter off her mind.

"All she does is nag, nag, nag!" Melissa complained. "I couldn't believe how my mother was hassling me to clean up my bedroom before I left this morning. And Dad was going along with her. For Pete's sake! Saturday is my only day off."

Sherri laughed as Melissa began to give a "live" imitation of her mother's lecture. Melissa pursed her lips together tightly and laid her drying cloth across her head. "Now, young lady," she said, wagging her finger at Sherri, "you probably think you should have a good time once in a while! No way!"

Trying to ignore his sister, Mark spotted a red car just out of the car wash. Behind the wheel was a frightened-looking Augustine.

"Hey, Mr. Augustine," Mark said, as Augustine rolled the window down. "You okay?"

"More terrifying than a shipwreck!" gasped Augustine, who looked a little closer to his reported age.

"Well," Mark said, "pull over there. We're here to help earn money for handicapped children. We get part of the car-wash profits. We'll dry the *red rocket* off for you."

Wearing a jacket over a flannel shirt and corduroys, Augustine had stepped out of the car and stood talking to Mark.

Gradually, Augustine noticed Melissa — still on stage at the car wash. Augustine seemed to understand "the plot" in an instant. Mark saw that a sad expression suddenly spread across his well-tanned face.

So You Think It's Tough Being a Teenager

For the moment, no more cars were in the car wash, and Augustine insisted on buying Cokes for Mark and his other young friends. Since Memorial Park picnic tables were close by, the five sat down.

"Thanks, Mr. Augustine," Jesse said, downing his can in four healthy swigs. "It's kinda surprising to see you here at a car wash, but we're glad you came!"

"Well," said Augustine, unzipping his jacket, "I thought cars might be a little like us. We feel happier when we're clean and bright. Are you all pretty happy this morning?"

Melissa felt her face grow hot with embarrassment. But she stared down at the Coke she was still sipping, and her hair hung forward shielding her from the dark eyes.

From high above, two squirrels in one of the oak

trees seemed to be dropping down shells to break the silence. After a very long pause, Augustine began to speak.

"I remember," he said, "that I was very unhappy when I made my mother unhappy." The voice was now mysterious, betraying that strange accent the four sometimes noticed.

Melissa's eyes lifted to find Augustine's black eyes on her. But Augustine's look was kind, understanding. The shame and embarrassment about mocking her mother left her.

"I tried to ignore the fact that I felt bad when I made my mother sad. I told myself that she didn't understand me," Augustine continued. "I knew that I was intelligent, and I believed that excused my disobedience. I had a lot of pride then — when I was young."

None of them bothered to ask how Augustine knew that Melissa had quarreled with her mother that morning. There was such an honesty to Augustine, to the way he spoke.

"But my parents can be so unreasonable at times," Melissa said softly in a pleading tone.

"Mine too," agreed Jesse.

"Yeah, I think my mother and father are wrong a lot too," added Juanita. "Even if they are divorced, that's no excuse for them to be so mean to each other. And they don't seem to realize how that hurts me. Sometimes I think that all they care about is themselves."

"Well," added Augustine, draining his can of the last precious swallow of Coke, "it would be nice to have parents who were . . . perfect. However, there is only one parent who is perfect."

"God, the Father?" interrupted Juanita.

"Yes," agreed Augustine, angling his face now to catch the sunlight breaking through the oaks. "And it's not even easy to love and obey a perfect Father, is it?"

The Gift of Reverence

"But at Confirmation," he said, "the Holy Spirit gives us another gift called reverence. This gift was often called piety in the past.

"Being able to recognize and revere God as Father really is a gift," Augustine said. "Jesus, who was God's only Son, told us that God is our Father too. He told us to practice thinking of God as Father when he taught us the Our Father. He even said that we should call God *Abba,* or 'Daddy.'

"But there is a Scripture story that gives us an even better picture of this gift of reverence," Augustine said. "It is about the time Jesus was separated from his parents at Passover in Jerusalem."

"I remember," added Melissa eagerly. "Mary and Joseph found Jesus back in the Temple answering the toughest questions the teachers could think of."

"That's right," laughed Augustine. "That story gives us a good look at the gift of reverence. First, Jesus told his parents: 'Did you not know I had to be in my Father's house?'[1] In other words, it was only natural for the Son of God to be showing reverence for his Father in the Temple.

"But then," added Augustine, "the Bible tells us that Jesus 'went down with them then, and came to Nazareth, and was obedient to them.'[2] Jesus also revered his earthly parents and their authority. And Jesus was God with a human mother and a human foster father! The Fourth Commandment tells us to . . ."

"Honor your father and your mother," his four young friends broke in all together.

"Hmmmm," Augustine intoned, stroking his chin.

"I guess you've already heard that."

"Oh, once a week — if it's a slow week," responded Melissa, teasingly rather than out of anger. They all laughed heartily, and Augustine joined in with them.

"My young friends!" Augustine said, looking up to the sky. "What an awesome power God has given parents to create life. But what an awesome responsibility he has given them to nurture that life. You know, we revere God because he is God, because of the gift of his Son, because of his promise of eternal life. We owe it to him! So we should revere our parents because they are parents, because of the sacrifices they make, and because of the promise they make to provide care and love. We owe it to them."

"Doesn't sound like the real world to me," Jesse responded.

"Ah, yes," Augustine smiled. "God is perfect, but parents are full of imperfections. You learned that when you first grew out of childhood." His words drew smiles of agreement from his listeners. "Sometimes our parents are weak and unsure, so out of respect, we provide help. And sometimes they make mistakes, and out of respect, we forgive them. But as to reverence — we owe it to them."

We Are Children of Light

"Reverence, reverence, my young friends," Augustine said, his eyes now squinting against the noonday sun. "Pray for the power of this grace. God really wants us to revere him. And he wants us to revere our parents. But God's expectations don't stop there. His eyes are much wider than ours. He also wants us to respect all of his creation: all human life, even all plant life and the birds, the fish, and the beasts as well."

No sooner had the last word left his mouth when half of an acorn shell smacked the table an inch from Augustine's right hand.

"And squirrels!" Augustine yelled, laughing and looking up into the oaks.

Jesse and Mark thought the squirrel's message was hilarious. Melissa almost knocked over her Coke trying to find the guilty squirrel. It was funny how events often seemed to help Augustine make his points — at just the right moment.

"Squirrels obviously try to protect their image," chuckled Augustine. "God protected us with laws he gave us to use his creation in the right way."

"Are you talking about the Commandments?" asked Juanita.

"They certainly are a good starting point, aren't they," Augustine answered.

"The Fifth Commandment says: *You shall not kill,*" Augustine said quietly, "but it also forbids any intentional harm done to others or to ourselves. The other Commandments also protect us."

"That's easy to see," grinned Jesse. "The Seventh Commandment, *You shall not steal,* and the Tenth, *You shall not covet your neighbor's goods,* have just protected Melissa."

"What do you mean?" Melissa demanded, turning to Jesse.

Grinning, Jesse pointed to the Coke can in front of her. When she'd turned her back, he'd swapped his empty can for hers.

"I forgive you," Melissa laughed, taking back her half-filled can.

"Well, I'm glad you are taking it all to heart," laughed Augustine. "Of course, the Eighth Commandment protects truth and individual reputations by telling us: *You shall not bear false witness against your neighbor.*

"Do you know which Commandments we haven't mentioned?" Augustine asked.

"One of them is *You shall not commit adultery*," Juanita quickly responded.

"The other," Jesse added, "is *You shall not covet your neighbor's wife*."

"The Sixth and Ninth Commandments, right?" Mark asked, not quite sure.

"You're all correct," Augustine said.

"But we're not married," Melissa objected, "so they don't really apply to us." Jesse and Mark nodded in agreement. Juanita looked skeptical.

"Ah, my young friends," Augustine exclaimed. "Your memory is correct, but your understanding needs building up. The Sixth and Ninth Commandments are important to your lives *right now*."

Augustine paused for a moment. "You're told by society, 'If it feels good, do it.' Sometimes you hear it openly. Other times the message comes in subtle disguises. But with so much teenage pregnancy and the many sexually transmitted diseases, you're also told, 'Do it *carefully!*' It seems as if very few people will tell you, 'Don't do it!' "

Augustine pretended not to notice the suppressed snickers of his friends. "The Sixth and Ninth Commandments," he continued, "strengthen you in the virtue of chastity. Chastity is an attitude of purity of heart that will help you to say no to sex too soon."

"It's hard . . . for some

kids," Melissa broke in sheepishly.

"Yes, I know, I know," Augustine said with a warm and understanding smile. "I was surprised to see your world about as amoral and sex-centered as Rome was in my day. But still, followers of Christ must learn to live a chaste life different from their pagan surroundings. And then as now, chastity is not without its rewards. Not only does chastity protect you from harm and pain, but it helps you to develop a respectful, nourishing attitude toward others. Chastity does something else that is very important. It pleases God. And God will richly bless you for trying to please him."

'God will richly bless you for trying to please him.'

"You see," said Augustine, "the Commandments provide a framework to respect the dignity and rights of people — to make life good. If we can respect one another's rights, possessions, and reputations, then we can build on that and grow in goodness and generosity. We can reach out for true justice, honoring God's creation the way you're doing here today."

"By washing cars?" asked Jesse, scratching his head.

"No, Dummy, by helping the handicapped," answered Mark. He patted Jesse's head as if he were an amusing three-year-old.

"Well," agreed Augustine, "I am very impressed with the way you have turned out to raise funds for the needy. That really is carrying reverence to its proper conclusion."

Melissa's Reconciliation

"Speaking of raising funds, we really should be getting back to wash some cars," suggested Mark, rising from the picnic table.

"Whoopee!" shouted Jesse, pointing toward the street. "Looks like a hundred cars are lined up!"

"Yeah, and our mom is first in line," said Mark, waving wildly to Mrs. McIntyre. Then Mark turned to face his sister. "Wasn't Mom going to a big bridge tournament today?"

"Yes," said Melissa shyly, looking down, "but she must have talked the rest of the ladies into coming here first."

"That was really good of her," remarked Augustine, turning to find Melissa's blue eyes. Mark, Jesse, and Juanita ran over to the McIntyre car where Mrs. McIntyre was just pulling into the car wash.

Only Melissa remained — seated directly across from Augustine. Melissa knew that if she went back to the car wash her mother would be there, and she felt a little uneasy. Augustine's eyes were gleaming with some kind of ancient mischief, a mysterious wisdom.

"I really know nothing about bridge," Augustine said, folding his arms, "but I bet I know what your mother would like better than good cards this afternoon."

"A good kid?" quipped Melissa. Suddenly, her anger and embarrassment were gone.

"Ah, you're such a bright child, a promising child!" Augustine laughed so long that Melissa began to blush. She rose quickly, grabbed her Coke, and smiled a thank you over her shoulder.

Augustine watched from under the oaks as Melissa ran to the water-beaded car coming out of the car wash. The window rolled down and a woman's arms reached out to hug a young girl leaning into the car.

---

[1] Luke 2.49.
[2] *Ibid.*, 2.51.

A Young Teen's Book of Catholic Knowledge

1. What does it mean to give reverence to God?

It means to see God as Father and to be grateful for the life he has given us and for his law, which guides us.

2. Why do we give reverence to God?

We reverence God because he is God — because of his boundless goodness and mercy — and because of the gift of life, the gift of his Son, and the promise of eternal life.

3. How did Jesus show reverence?

He obeyed God, his heavenly Father, in all things, even to suffering and dying for us. As a boy, he also obeyed Mary and Joseph, his mother and foster father.

4. How does the gift of reverence strengthen us?

It helps us to be grateful to God for his gifts to us. It helps us to respect all of God's children and all of God's creation and the laws God gave us so that we could have good relationships with others.

5. How do we know we have been open to the gift of reverence?

We will grow in goodness, kindness, and generosity.

6. How do we respect our parents?

We respect our parents by obeying them, helping them when they need us, listening to them when we need to hear a voice of authority, and forgiving them when they make mistakes.

7. How do we respect other people by observing the Fifth Commandment?

We turn away from violence and toward peacefulness.

8. How do we respect other people by obeying the Sixth and Ninth Commandments?

We act with modesty and chastity and seek to avoid occasions of impurity.

9. How do we respect other people by observing the Seventh and Tenth Commandments?

We do not take or scheme to take what belongs to others.

10. How do we respect other people by obeying the Eighth Commandment?

We tell the truth so that we can be trusted, and we do not say things that will harm the reputation of others.

11. What is our obligation to other people?

Our obligation to other people is to treat them with dignity and value by giving them their due and protecting their rights.

St. Martin de Porres

Illustration
by Alex Moore

By permission of
the Josephite
Pastoral Center,
Washington, D.C.

Martin de Porres did not grow up to be a bitter, angry man. That in itself was a small miracle. Life had cheated him of many things in childhood.

Martin was the son of a white Spanish nobleman and a black woman from Panama who had once been a slave. Martin's parents had fallen in love, but Juan would not marry Anna because of her race. When Martin was born in 1579 in Lima, Peru, Juan de Porres was disappointed that the boy's skin and features were like his mother's. After a dark-skinned little girl was born, Juan left them. From time to time, he sent a little money but not enough to protect Anna and the children from hunger and real need.

And so, Martin's mother worked constantly just to keep them alive. Martin also saw that his black mother resented him as much as his white father did. Anna believed that Martin's black skin was the reason Juan left her. In the middle of so much rejection, the boy became even more loving, more generous. Though his own family had little to eat, Martin often gave away bread. His mother punished him. But the boy could not resist giving to those who were hungrier than he was.

By his teenage years, Martin had been taught to be a barber. In those days, this work also included medical training. By the time he was fifteen, he was very experienced at minor surgery, setting bones, tending to wounds, and mixing medications. But Martin knew that God was calling him to religious life. He became a Dominican lay brother and was given only cleaning jobs to do. Martin didn't mind the humble work. When it was done, he was often found at prayer.

Eventually, Martin's healing gifts were put to good use. He took care of the sick Dominicans. They noticed that remarkable cures took place when the prayerful Brother Martin cared for them. Others also heard about his gifts. Soon, the poor and sick of Lima lined up outside the Dominican house.

Martin began to spend more and more time helping the poor. Rising evey morning at 4 A.M. to greet the dawn, he spent his days tending to the city's sick and hungry. He distributed food and money. He cared for the sick. He started the Orphanage of the Holy Cross which was still in existence in modern times. His own experience of being unwanted may explain Martin's concern for others.

Brother Martin died at the age of sixty in 1639. Many stories were already being told about his great reverence for all of God's creation. His love for the Father who had always wanted him led him to give everything to the poor, including himself.

The same Gospel of brotherly love that inspired St. Martin still inspires ministries of caring today like this medical and dental clinic.

Ten Reasons to Give Reverence to Our Father

The first reason we give reverence to the Father is simply because he is God, because of his boundless goodness and mercy. But we owe him reverence because of his many gifts to us. The crossword below mentions 10 gifts — some of the best reasons to give reverence to the Father. Read the clues and figure them out.

ACROSS

1. It's called the People of God, the Mystical Body of Christ.

2. He so loved the world that he gave this.

3. What Christians are called to proclaim.

4. His first gift to us.

5. If we believe in Jesus, we will have this.

6. In the letter of James, we are told that this is "sown in peace for those who cultivate peace" (James 4.18).

DOWN

7. What God is in 1 John 4.8.

8. We will receive power from this.

9. If we had this the size of a mustard seed, we could move mountains.

10. John the Baptizer told us to repent of our sins and to seek this.

What happens if we don't open these gifts? Or if we open them, but never do anything with them?

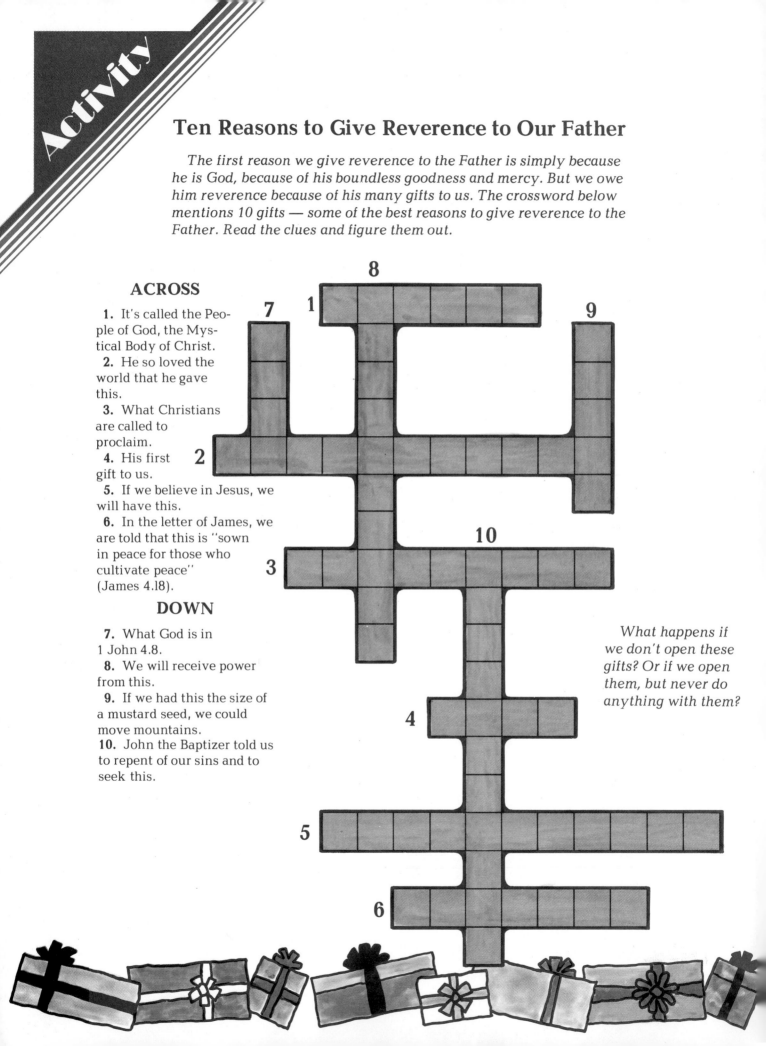

Steps to Discipleship

Around A.D. 51 or 52, shortly after his second missionary journey, St. Paul wrote his first letter to the Christians of Thessalonica, a city in Greece. Paul wrote a similar letter to the Romans about A.D. 57 and pleaded with them to keep the faith. In both letters, Paul suggested ways of Christian living, some of which are listed below in Column A. In Column B, you will find examples of these ways of Christian living. Match the action that fits with the code of behavior.

Column A

1 ___ Detest what is evil.

2 ___ Be fervent in spirit, for he whom you serve is the Lord.

3 ___ Be patient under trial.

4 ___ Persevere in prayer.

5 ___ Associate with those who are humble.

6 ___ Never repay injury with injury.

7 ___ Respect those in authority over you.

8 ___ Remain at peace with one another.

9 ___ Admonish the unruly.

10 ___ Support those who are timid.

11 ___ Be pure, not like the pagans, and grow in holiness.

Column B

A. Although many of his classmates were silent when the prayers were said during Mass, Paul said them with enthusiasm and commitment.

B. Mike wasn't sure in his heart that God listened to him when he prayed, but he stuck with it even when he didn't feel like doing it.

C. Sean was stung by someone who insulted him, but he turned away and did not get angry.

D. Rikki didn't care for some of the students in her class, but since they were going to be spending a lot of time together, she tried to get along with everyone.

E. Kristie noticed that Tom, who was a good singer, shied away from joining the chorus. So she encouraged him constantly to join in.

F. When asked how she felt about cheating, Susan said it was wrong, even though she knew that some of her friends cheated often.

G. Laurie was upset with her parents when they grounded her, unfairly she felt, but she obeyed their commands in hope of winning their trust.

H. Although Susan found Diane exciting in some ways, she didn't like the way Diane showed off and bragged about herself. Instead Susan befriended another girl who was quiet and unassuming.

I. Shelley and Lisa thought a homework assignment given by their teacher was too much, but they refrained from making any sassy remarks about their teacher to friends.

J. Mark told John that his nasty comments to a homely-looking girl were wrong and that John should stop acting that way.

K. Bill told Brian that even if the world around us seems to be in a sex-mess, many Christians still try to do their part by leading chaste lives.

Chapter 5

The Powerful Gift of Courage

Some Special People at St. Jude's

"Come on, Jess'. Let's go, buddy!" Mark called out the window of Augustine's car.

Augustine, the McIntyres, and Juanita had just pulled up in front of the Hamilton house. It was a chilly Thursday afternoon. Jesse sat chin in hand on the front steps. He looked a bit sad as he jogged down the sidewalk and grabbed the door to swing in next to Mark and Melissa in the back.

After the car wash, Augustine had offered to take the four to St. Jude's Hospital. The young people would be able to see the work being done for handicapped children, the children they had raised money for. Mark, Melissa, Jesse, and Juanita had all agreed to it right away. But now that they were headed for the hospital, the four lively teens had nothing to say. Their early enthusiasm was gone.

"Mr. Augustine," said Juanita, finally breaking the silence. "What will these children be like? I know they are kids like us. But will they seem a little . . . scary at first?"

"Hmmm," responded Augustine. One quick glance in the rearview mirror at the others told the story. They were all anxiously awaiting the answer to Juanita's question. In this century, Augustine reminded himself, the handicapped were often out of sight, almost invisible. As a result, there was often a fear of the handicapped.

"Some of the handicapped children you will see are not beautiful," said Augustine. "But God has given them other gifts. I want you to look closely. Don't be afraid. You will see some beautiful things today."

Once inside the massive red-brick hospital, Mark, Melissa, Juanita, and Jesse were introduced to Dr. Sebastian Miller, the director. There in the lobby, a four-year-old black girl crawled over to Jesse and threw her arms around his legs. Her own legs were wrapped in steel braces from the ankles to the waist. Jesse looked down into the smiling little face and wondered what to do.

"Isn't she darling!" gasped Melissa. She and Juanita stooped down to pat the little girl's head and straighten her shirt.

"That's Rachel," laughed Dr. Miller, "She wears the leg braces because she has a crippling disease called cerebral palsy. But she's also retarded and thinks that every young black fellow is her older brother, Cliff. What she'd really like is to have you pick her up, Jesse."

Something seemed to melt in Jesse's heart. He leaned down and picked up the grinning little girl. Her steel-braced legs clanged together as he lifted her. She was lighter than his little sister, Deborah.

"Tiff, Tiff," Rachel squealed with delight. Jesse grinned and felt happier than he had since Monday.

"Let's go down the hall, and I'll give you the tour," suggested Dr. Miller.

The Spirit Is No Cowardly Spirit

At a room labeled "Physical Therapy," Augustine and the four stopped in front of a large one-way glass viewing window. Holding onto parallel bars beyond the window was an older girl of about eight. She wore her hair in pigtails and stood inside leg braces similar to Rachel's. On a chair waiting and watching was a little boy in braces.

As Dr. Miller, Augustine, and the four stood and watched, the therapist helped the girl. She was learning to swing out one leg, balance, and then swing out the other. All the while, the girl held tightly to the bars. When she got to the end, a big smile flashed across her face.

"I did it. I got to the end!" she laughed. The therapist leaned over and wrapped the girl in a big hug.

"That's Carrie," commented Dr. Miller. "Like Rachel, she has cerebral palsy, but she has normal intelligence. Right now, Carrie is finding it very hard to walk, but she's a fighter! Next, the therapist will begin to teach her to walk without the help of the parallel bars. But let's go down to the end of the hall. We have a boy in therapy down there who's a few years older than you. His name is Steve Bailey."

"Is that the Steve Bailey who was a quarterback at Northside?" inquired Jesse.

"That's right," said Dr. Miller. "You probably remember that he was injured in an auto accident two years ago. He was paralyzed from the waist down. He comes in to work out to strengthen his arm and chest muscles. I'm sure he'd like to meet you.

"Steve, have you got a minute for a few visitors?" Dr. Miller called into a large room filled with gym and exercise equipment.

A young man with blond hair was seated on a mat. Bracing himself with one arm, he pulled a weight on a pulley with the other arm.

"Sure," Steve called out instantly. He let the weight drop slowly and then swung his body around. On his belly, the handsome young man calmly scooted over to a nearby wheelchair, dragging his legs behind him. With a motorized lift, he raised himself to the seat level of the wheelchair and moved over onto it.

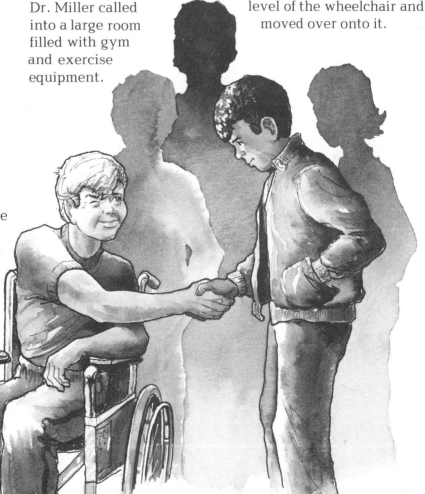

"Pleased to meet you," said Steve. There was an easy grin and bright blue eyes behind the shock of blond hair. He stretched his hand out to Mark and Jesse and then to Augustine and the girls. Then, the hand went out again to Jesse.

"Got a pretty good grip, fella," Steve winked up at Jesse. "You into sports?"

"Well," mumbled Jesse, "I play some football like you . . . I mean . . . ."

"Like I used to?" interrupted Steve, aware of Jesse's discomfort. "Well, football days are over for every guy sooner or later. Now I work out here by myself three times a week. Otherwise, I spend my time with computers. Hope to go to college next year!"

There was pride in the young man's voice. He was proud of his accomplishments. What's more, he was determined to persist.

"Isn't that guy some example of real courage." Out in the hallway, Dr. Miller shook his head in amazement "Steve's patience and courage," he said, "helped every child at the hopsital. And if you'd been with him a little longer, you would have found that Steve has a very deep religious faith. That's what keeps him going."

Forty-five minutes later,

Augustine and the four teens were walking slowly down the hospital sidewalk toward the parking lot. After leaving Steve, they had gone on to visit other therapy rooms and some severely retarded children in a playroom.

"I'm sorry I was afraid of coming here," said Juanita, looking up at Augustine. "These children are so patient, so good!"

"Yeah, and how about that Steve!" added Mark. "The guy has really gone through some tough things, and he can still manage to smile and make jokes."

"Well . . ." agreed Augustine, "I think we all learned something about perseverance." He pointed his thumb over his shoulder toward the red-brick building behind them. "You saw children struggling with their crooked or useless legs trying to do things that they see other people do without even thinking.

'You live in a time of much violence. So did I.'

"But everyone will have difficulties and trials to face in this life. You, too, my friends, can expect to have many crosses in your lives,

including 'the regulars' — pain and aging and death. But when any trial comes along, you can draw much strength from what St. Peter said about suffering. Would you believe he actually told us to be *glad* to share in the sufferings of Christ, because when Christ comes in glory, we will be filled with joy.[1] It's very deep and not easy to understand, but it is true.

"But we have more to talk about, and we can do that as we drive along."

Draw Your Strength From the Lord

Augustine circled the car and unlocked all four doors on the little "red rocket." The twins, Jesse and Juanita, climbed in quietly. Augustine slipped into the driver's seat, put the key in the ignition and then drove onto the street.

"There was a gift of the Holy Spirit that I wanted you to see today," Augustine said softly. "What do you suppose it was?"

"I don't know what it's called, but I bet it had something to do with guts," said Jesse. He was sitting sideways to give his bigger frame extra room in Augustine's tiny back seat.

"Yes," agreed Augustine, smiling warmly at Jesse. "It

is called the gift of courage. And it's such an important gift! When you are confirmed, this powerful gift of grace will be strengthened in you. It will help you persist in times of trial. At the same time, it helps to relieve you of the fear and anxiety you may feel during times of difficulty.

'I bet it had something to do with guts.'

"Remember the story of St. Paul?" Augustine continued. His face was getting that look of excitement once again. His eyes flickered with points of fire.

"Uh huuuh . . ." Melissa and Mark answered together in perfect twin timing. Jesse and Juanita had seen it happen dozens of times. Augustine just shook his head in amazement.

"Well," Augustine said, picking up his thoughts. "Paul suffered in so many ways. Shipwreck, imprisonment, beatings, hunger, the loss of friends, persecution, and finally, death by beheading. He understood the need for courage as few do. Where did he find such courage to persist?

"In his letter to the Ephesians, Paul said: 'draw your strength from the Lord and his mighty power. Put on the armor of God so that you may be able to stand firm against the tactics of the devil'.[1] In short, Paul said that courage is given by God and that the real need for courage is against the evils of the world."

"Hey, yeah!" Jesse blurted out. "You mean like puchin' out the bad guys, like on TV?"

"You live in a time of much violence," Augustine added. "So did I. As the Roman Empire was collapsing, there was chaos and violence everywhere. But I'm not speaking of the courage that is propped up by swords, as it was in my time, or the awful weapons of your time. St. Paul said: 'Stand fast, with the *truth* as the belt around your waist, *justice* as your breastplate, and *zeal to propagate the gospel of peace* as your footgear.'[3] He said to hold *faith* as your shield, to take God's *promise of salvation* as your helmet, and the *word of God* as your sword."[4]

"Maybe today we should put more hope in the Word of God than in our nuclear weapons," Mark suggested.

"Very profound, Mark," Augustine responded. As he turned a corner, he apparently thought of something else. "You know, it isn't courageous or brave to do foolhardy or dangerous things like taking dares . . . or jumping off three-story buildings," Augustine reminded his four friends.

"Or like riding in the car while he's driving?" Melissa whispered to her brother.

Though Augustine couldn't figure why, the McIntyres were soon giggling in the back seat as the "red rocket" chugged down Division Street.

Be Strong and Be Reconciled to God

Augustine soon dropped off Juanita at the Sanchez residence. Juanita ran in, knowing her mother would appreciate help with dinner after her day at work. Jesse moved into the front seat where Juanita had been sitting. At the McIntyre house, the twins hurried out, swinging the car door shut behind them.

"Thanks, Mr. Augustine," Mark called out.

"Yes, it was really a good trip, Mr. Augustine," added Melissa. Her tone, Augustine noticed, was quite sincere for a change!

"Something troubling you, my young friend?" Augustine asked his remaining passenger.

Jesse stared at the man

driving the car. Augustine had not taken his eyes from the street. And yet he seemed to have looked right through Jesse to his core . . . to the thing Jesse was trying to hide and forget.

"Yes, sir," Jesse admitted. His chin fell to his chest. He felt almost sick, but the reason for the sickness quickly spilled out.

'Dishonesty will just weaken your inner self.'

"I cheated on a test last Monday, because I was afraid of failing math," Jesse confessed. "I didn't want to be dropped from the football team. I was a coward. I couldn't take my medicine and tough it out. When I met Steve Bailey today, I knew how wrong I was. He keeps on trying, and he can't even walk!"

"Believe me, Jesse," Augustine said gently, "I know what it feels like to finally look your mistakes in the face. It's not easy; it hurts."

"I don't know what to do," moaned Jesse, looking anxiously out his window.

"Couldn't you tell this to your teacher, just as you have told me?" asked Augustine calmly. He had

pulled into a parking lot where a gas station had once operated. Jesse, he knew, needed a little time to get it all out.

"Tell Mr. Cowley?" gasped Jesse. "He thinks I'm the type who would never cheat. He'll think that Jesse Hamilton is a no-good creep. And I'll get dropped from the team anyway."

"That may happen, and I it would be very sad for you," agreed Augustine. "St. Paul also said: 'By the might of his glory you will be endowed with the strength needed to stand fast.'[5] Football may help you build a strong body, Jesse, but living with your dishonesty will just weaken your inner self."

"I guess," said Jesse. The tone was a little less hopeless now. There was, instead, a certain hint of peace, a resignation to fight the fears he still had.

"Be strong. Make use of the gift of courage that you already have," urged Augustine. "If you let him, the Lord will see to it that it grows and is strengthened . . . just like Steve's muscles and courage, which so impressed you today. Shall I take you home now?"

"No," said Jesse. Finally, he lifted his head to look into those eyes that knew cowardice and courage in

ancient times.

"Could you drop me at the rectory?" Jesse asked. "I'll look up Father Mike. I'd like to talk to him and receive the Sacrament of Reconciliation before I talk to Mr. Cowley tomorrow." A smile broke once again on Jesse's face. "I always feel like a first-string tackle has just gotten off of me when I leave confession."

"Ha!" laughed Augustine. "I think I know what you mean. That's the way the Lord wants you to feel. Believe me, I know! In any case, the Lord wants you to receive Confirmation in the state of grace, so you're doing exactly what you should be doing."

Two minutes later, the little red car did a risky-looking U-turn on Division Street and headed back toward the tall spire of St. Ignatius Church.

[1] Based on 1 Peter 4.13.
[2] Ephesians 6.10-11.
[3] Ibid., 6.14-15.
[4] See Ibid., 6.16-17.
[5] Colossians 1.11.

A Young Teen's Book of Catholic Knowledge

1. **How does the gift of courage give us power?**

   It strengthens our faith by overcoming spiritual lukewarmness. It increases our commitment to witnessing the Gospel and to living a Christian life. It increases our resolve not to make excuses, give up, or quit during hard times.

2. **How do we know we have been open to the gift of courage?**

   We will grow in patience and composure during times of suffering.

3. **What is the greatest act of courage?**

   Martyrdom.

4. **What does courage oppose?**

   Cowardice and doing foolish things that give the appearance of courage.

5. **How does it take courage to tell the truth?**

   It is courageous to live according to God's truth when it is hard or unpopular.

6. **How does it take courage to live a life of justice?**

   It is courageous to stand up for someone else's rights, especially when it may require self-sacrifice, including the sacrifice of one's life.

7. **Is it courageous to live by faith?**

   Yes, it is courageous to make God number one when the world encourages you to live by materialistic goals and values.

8. **How does courage help us to be reconciled with God?**

   It helps us to admit our sinfulness, to say we're sorry, and to resolve to amend our lives.

9. **Why is the examination of conscience so important in the Sacrament of Reconciliation?**

   We must continually examine our life in order to realize the need for conversion. Without that realization, we cannot respond to our Lord's call to repentance.

10. **How does courage help us to deal with suffering and pain?**

    We live in a society that attempts to remove all suffering from life. Christ asks each of us at times to carry our crosses in union with him. Courage helps us to bear our sufferings as well as help others endure theirs.

11. **What are the requirements for receiving the Sacrament of Confirmation validly and fruitfully?**

    A person must be in the state of grace (free of any mortal sin), and if above the age of reason, must be taught about the sacrament and be willing to accept the responsibilities that go with it, namely, to bear witness to Christ in mature Christian living.

St Joan of Arc

At seventeen, she donned her battle armor.

Depictions of St. Joan by courtesy of the Sisters of St. Joan of Arc, Quebec.

She was barely a teenager when it all began to happen.

Born in January, 1412, she was the youngest of the five children of Jacques and Isabelle D'Arc, a farming couple of Domrémy in the northeast of France. During the spring when she was thirteen, Joan had a strange experience in the garden. She had always been very prayerful. But suddenly, a voice told her not to be afraid. It was the first of her visions. Soon, she realized that the voice was that of St. Michael the Archangel.

The next five years brought Joan many visions. These visions were of two virgin martyrs, St. Catherine of Alexandria and St. Margaret of Antioch. Gradually, Joan understood that she too should remain a virgin. She also learned that she would be given tasks to perform for God and France. She was to save the city of Orléans from the English. Then, she was to see that Charles, the French heir, was crowned king at Rheims.

For better than ninety years, France had been at war with England over title to lands in France. One French region, Burgundy, had sided with England against France. But, what was a country girl to do about all of that? She couldn't even read or write! And yet the gift of courage told her she could do something about it.

Joan cut her hair like a boy's, put on male clothing, and convinced Charles that she was sent by God. She had a battle banner made that carried the

At nineteen, her courageous mission was completed.

In 1430, Joan was captured. She had been expecting it. Her "voices" had told her that it would happen. At first, she was light-hearted about it all. But for a year, she was treated brutally. She was locked in irons in a dungeon where she was denied the Mass and sacraments.

Joan was tried for heresy and witchcraft rather than military crimes. King Charles made no attempt to save her. Her punishment, she knew, would be unbearably horrid. She was to be burned to death at the stake. Strong all through her trial, Joan defended what she had done. God and the saints had told her what to do, not the devil. However, toward the end of the trial, her great courage weakened. She admitted her "evil-doing" and denied her visions. Fear of the death and pain she was to face had weakened her.

But within a day or two, Joan realized that being saved by a lie was not worth it. Her conscience and her voices rebuked her. So, Joan told her captors that she stood again by her faith, her voices, and the truth. Her execution order was written.

On a spring morning in 1431, she was taken to the marketplace at Rouen in a cart. As she was being tied to a stake atop a large pile of wood, an English soldier made a cross out of some twigs for her. Soon, Joan watched the flames lick up higher and higher toward her. In pain, she cried out "Jesus, Jesus." As she died, one of the English soldiers insisted that he saw a white bird rise from the burning pyre and rise toward heaven. Joan was just nineteen.

The Church canonized Joan of Arc, as she is now known, in 1920. Her feast day was fixed on May 30, the day she faced the flames with courage and died.

words "Jesus Maria." Finally, the French heir believed her. Dressed in white armor, she told the French soldiers to prepare their souls for battle. In a wonderful victory, the city of Orléans was won back from the English in the spring of 1429. Other victories followed. Joan saw Charles VII crowned a few months later. But, despite Joan's victories, the French failed to make the most of them.

Steps to Discipleship

Sixty times in the New Testament there is found a call to repentance. Repentance is turning away from sin and turning toward God (Chapter 2). Before we can repent, we must examine the way we live. Courage helps us to do that honestly and to take the steps necessary to achieve repentance. Use the following Scripture citations to develop questions to examine your own conscience. The first one is provided as a sample.

Scripture Citation

1) Present your needs to God in every form of prayer and in petitions full of gratitude *(Philippians 4.6)*.

2) Respect those among you whose task it is to exercise authority in the Lord and admonish you *(1 Thessalonians 5.12)*.

3) I beg you to be on the watch against those who cause dissension and scandal. . . . Avoid their company *(Romans 16.17)*.

4) You must know that your body is a temple of the Holy Spirit. . . . So glorify God in your body *(1 Corinthians 6.19-20)*.

5) Do not return evil for evil or insult for insult *(1 Peter 3.9)*.

6) My brothers, what good is it to profess faith without practicing it? *(James 2.14)*.

7) Be patient toward all *(1 Thessalonians 5.14)*.

8) Do not continue in ignorance, but try to discern the will of the Lord *(Ephesians 5.17)*.

9) Forgive whatever grievances you have against one another *(Colossians 3.13)*.

10) In everything you do, act without grumbling or arguing *(Philippians 2.14)*.

11) Out of love, place yourselves at one another's service *(Galatians 5.13)*.

12) Realize that when your faith is tested this makes for endurance *(James 1.3)*.

Examination of Conscience

1) Do I _talk to God every day? Do I_ _worship God at Mass and not just sit there?_ _When I pray do I thank and praise God?_

2) Do I _____

3) Do I _____

4) Do I _____

5) Do I _____

6) Do I _____

7) Do I _____

8) Do I _____

9) Do I _____

10) Do I _____

11) Do I _____

12) Do I _____

Circle the one that you have to work on the hardest.

Chapter 6

The Powerful Gift of Right Judgment

A Special Visitor

"Well, I'm really glad to hear about all of your confirmation lessons," smiled a well-built white-haired man. He sported a bushy mustache and looked at Mark with a joyful light in his bright blue eyes. The eyes, Mark noticed once again, were so much like his mother's.

For the McIntyres, this was a special Friday afternoon. Grandpa Foster had come to visit his youngest daughter and her family. He had arrived late in the morning and was waiting for the twins and their seven-year-old sister, Sally, when they came home from school.

Mark, in particular, loved these visits. Captain John J. ("Jack") Foster had been a pilot and a war hero in the South Pacific during World War II. As he always did when he came, Grandpa sat in the recliner in the McIntyres' study. He put up his right leg, which still often ached from a war injury. After the war, Jack Foster had become a commercial airline pilot. He'd flown all over

the world and had many stories. But the story he was telling wasn't from flying days.

"I remember my own Confirmation," said Grandpa Foster. "That night, I walked out toward the barn and looked up at the stars. I was thinking of what we had been taught about the first Pentecost — about the tongues of fire. The more I looked at the stars, the more

I thought of those tongues of fire lit by the Holy Spirit. I could still feel the oil wet on my forehead. Suddenly, I felt different in a way I couldn't describe. Maybe that was boyish imagination, but I believed that I had really received a fresh, mighty dose of the Holy Spirit that day."

"Did it last?" Mark asked. He was fascinated by the distant vision of a Kansas farm boy sensing the presence of the Holy Spirit.

"Well, no," admitted Grandpa Foster. "Like most people, I got involved in day-to-day things, and the feeling wore off. As I got older, I guess I became just an ordinary believer. I got quite attached to the way things were done in the Church, for instance, the way Masses were said. Mass was said in Latin back then, you know. But to be honest, I never thought much about it. Do you know when I really started to think about it again?"

"No . . ." Mark started to say.

Melissa rushed into the study. "Mark! You won't believe what Dad said!" Her face was red with emotion. Her dark hair looked wild and wind-blown. Melissa's voice told her twin that she couldn't decide whether she should cry or scream.

Grandpa Foster looked up with concern.

"What's up?" Mark insisted.

"Mom just told me that Dad isn't going to let us go to Steve's party tonight?"

"Why?" demanded Mark angrily. "He already said we could go."

"I don't know!" Melissa said, stamping her foot with frustration. "Mom wouldn't explain. Juanita's mother called last night and talked with Mom. Afterward, Mom talked to Dad. Then, he decided that the party wouldn't be good for us." Melissa's voice had picked up that mocking tone.

"Now, young lady," Grandpa Foster interrupted, "your dad knows what is best for you."

"Ha!" responded Melissa. "He doesn't even know what's best for himself! He smokes cigarettes like a chimney! But he's going to have a choice to make about that next week."

Behind Melissa, the slim figure of Jean McIntyre suddenly stood in the study doorway.

"I'm sorry, Dad!" the twins' mother whispered to her father over her daughter's head. "Melissa," she said calmly, turning the girl around by her shoulders, "why don't you cool off in your bedroom?"

"Good idea," fumed Melissa; "maybe I can get my temperature down to about a thousand!"

In a moment, Mark and his grandfather were alone again. "What did Melissa mean about your dad having a choice to make about smoking next week?" Grandpa Foster finally asked. "Can you tell me, or is it a secret?"

"Well," explained Mark, "it is sort of a secret, but I guess I can tell you. Melissa and I have been learning in science class about the risks of smoking. We told Dad about them, but he doesn't seem to be worried. Then, Melissa read an article in the newspaper about a boycott. She had this idea that we should boycott eating breakfasts until Dad quits smoking. See, he's always saying that breakfast is the most important meal of the day."

"I see, I see . . ." nodded Grandpa Foster smiling to himself. Mark watched the smile spread across the tanned, wrinkled face. Was his grandfather thinking of things his own children had done? Mark got up, lightly patted Grandpa's wounded leg, and headed to his room.

"See you later, son," Grandpa grinned. "Your secret is safe with me."

Right Judgment and Ice-cream Sodas

It was Saturday, and Melissa and Mark were treating Grandpa to lunch at Bonnie Doyle's ice-cream shop downtown. A little after noon, Mark and Melissa proudly escorted their grandfather into Bonnie Doyle's. "Oh, wow, look!" laughed Melissa, slapping her cheek with surprise. As they turned around from the coat rack, she spotted the smiling faces of Jesse, Juanita, and Augustine! They were waving wildly at them from the opposite side of the restaurant.

"Grandpa, would you mind if we join some friends for lunch today?" Mark asked.

"Why no," beamed Jack Foster, "I'd love to meet your friends. But I presume that the older guy is not one of your classmates!"

"No, but you could say that he's in a class by himself," joked Melissa. "That's Mr. Augustine. A lot of people think he's a real saint!"

"I hear that you are helping these youngsters to prepare for Confirmation," Grandpa Foster said, extending his hand to Augustine.

"With God's help," agreed Augustine.

The two older men sat together. Soon, they were talking as though they'd been next-door neighbors for life. Jack Foster asked Augustine what business

he'd been in and where he had lived. But with every answer Augustine gave, Jack was getting more and more confused.

"At the party last night, Steve was passing around some stuff. Got my drift?" whispered Jesse to Mark, who was sitting next to him at the end of the table. Melissa leaned toward Mark to catch the conversation while Juanita told Grandpa Foster about their school activities.

"Weren't Steve's parents there?" asked Mark quietly. "He said they would be. That's why we were able to talk Mom and Dad into it."

"They were supposed to be . . ." agreed Jesse, shrugging his shoulders.

Sodas, hamburger platters, and sundaes had arrived. Augustine pushed back his chair. He blinked repeatedly at the double chocolate soda Juanita had suggested that he order.

"I'm not convinced that this is the right day to talk about the gift of right judgment," Augustine said, staring at the untouched soda in front of him. "That's the gift of the Holy Spirit that guides us to make correct decisions. Looks as if all this bubbly stuff would go straight to the brain!"

"Well, I don't think sodas scramble the brain the way

some other things we know about," said Jesse, winking at Mark.

Augustine looked at Jesse as though he'd read his mind. He let his fries and hamburger lie on the plate but pulled the soda suspiciously toward him. Two slurps confirmed the virtues of double chocolate sodas. Augustine's face had the look of a man who'd made a wonderful discovery.

eliminating certain people from your list of possible husbands?" asked Melissa, giggling at Juanita across the table.

"Yes," agreed Augustine, "and friends, too. Or what to allow or forbid your children to do."

For a second, Melissa's face turned a color not so different from the cherry soda in front of her. But she

low the Lord, the more this gift is available to us."

"Amen," added Grandpa Foster. "But doesn't the Church also use right judgment, or counsel as we used to call it?"

"Absolutely," agreed Augustine. He saw that Jack Foster had something to share.

"Right judgment, or counsel, as it is also called, is a gift of the Holy Spirit and a gift of power, or grace, like the others," began Augustine. "This gift leads us to make decisions that are guided by the Holy Spirit. It also opens us to take direction from others, the right others, as we get to those points where we must make the right choices."

"You mean decisions like

said nothing. These young people no longer puzzled over how this man did or knew the things he did. Augustine politely ignored her embarrassment.

"For parents," continued Augustine, "the gift of right judgment may help them to protect their children from dangers the children just don't see. The more we fol-

The Church Is Spirit-Filled Too

"I started to tell Mark about this yesterday," said Grandpa Foster, "but . . . something came up."

"When I was a young man, I got busy with my career and courted the twins' grandmother Kathleen," began Grandpa Foster. "My religious interests sort of ended. Lots of years went by. Kathleen and I had grown children when the Second Vatican Council was taking place. For many, the changes in the Church were exciting. I thought they were a disaster. Everything was changed, ruined. I got angry. I quit going to church, but Kathleen didn't. She would tell me about what was going on, even though I pretended not to listen.

"A year after Kathleen died, I went back," admitted the twins' grandfather. "I knew that Kathleen wanted me to. After a few months, I could see that Mother Church was right. She had used this gift of right judgment. Hearing the Mass in English was beautiful. Seeing the priest say the Mass with his face to the people made me feel closer to Christ. I could see that the right choices had been made. I'm happy now about the changes."

Augustine smiled and clapped his new friend on the back. There was silence for a moment. The man who had just braved his first double chocolate soda now pushed his empty glass back with a look of longing. The waitress arrived to clear off the table. Augustine grabbed his plate with the cold hamburger and fries he hadn't been able to eat yet.

"You are so right, Jack," agreed Augustine. "The Church guides her children down through the ages with right judgment. Like a good parent, she depends upon the gathered wisdom of years and guides her children with this gift of the Spirit.

"And the Church helps us to discern truth from lies," Augustine continued, "to know what belongs to God and what belongs to the Evil One. In St. Matthew's Gospel, we are told: 'Be on your guard against false prophets, who come to you in sheep's clothing but underneath are wolves on the prowl.' "[1]

"I guess Jesse can tell us about such a wolf dressed in sheep's clothing, can't you?" Juanita asked knowingly.

"Yeah, I guess so," Jesse responded nervously. "You'll know them by their deeds, right?"

"Right, indeed! Excellent, Jesse," Augustine said applauding. "In fact, you took the words right out of St. Matthew's Gospel. And St. John in his First Epistle offered another way of knowing the spirit of truth from the spirit of deception. He said that anyone who belongs to God will be open to God's word, while anyone who is not of God refuses to hear or abide by God's word.

"In the Scriptures, right judgment is also pointed to as a gift that will be given to Christians in trouble," Augustine continued. "St. Mark quotes Jesus giving advice about this to his Apostles. The Lord told his followers: 'When men take you off into custody, do not worry beforehand about what to say. In that hour, say what you are inspired to say. It will not be yourselves speaking but the Holy Spirit.' "[2]

'The Church helps us to discern truth from lies.'

"Do you mean like the things St. Stephen said in Jerusalem?" asked Jesse.

"Yeah, but he got stoned right after he said those things!" complained Melissa.

Augustine and Jack Foster laughed heartily. They could see that Melissa was worried about what such a gift might lead to. At an earlier meeting, Augustine told Jack, the four had read the story about the martyrdom of Stephen in the Acts of the Apostles.

"In a usual way, for most Christians, right judgment protects us from unwise choices or from going in the wrong direction," Augustine said, trying to reassure Melissa. "But taking the wrong direction can also be dangerous, or it may simply result in confusion. Do you remember that the Hebrews wandered in the desert for forty years before reaching the Promised Land? As it says in the Psalms, these people 'forgot his works; they waited not for his counsel.' "[3]

"So, is right judgment just like knowing the right answer?" Jesse asked, scratching his head.

"Well, in a way," nodded Augustine. "But it isn't like punching in the numbers and getting the right answer on a calculator, or computer. Your heart has to be right even to see the right direction. Recognizing our weaknesses and our dependence on the Holy Spirit prepares us to have that clear vision, that ability to see the way the Lord wants us to take. Humility, patience, and right judgment make good partners."

Mark and Melissa Counsel Their Father

Augustine could see that he alone had food left to eat at the table. He reached for the bottle of ketchup but let his right hand pause for just a moment above the food. As he picked up the bottle and unscrewed the top, steam was suddenly rising from his plate.

"Look!" pointed Juanita. "Your burger and fries! They're hot again!"

"Oh," laughed Augustine, as though surprised. "Probably all that hot air I'm famous for! I was a teacher for many years, you know," he told Jack Foster. But like the others, Grandpa Foster was wide-eyed. For a few moments, no one had anything to say.

"Wellmph," Augustine said, trying to break the silence with a mouth full of burger, "wmhat are chew all dooin thisth afternooth?"

"I'm going to write a nice letter to Dad," said Melissa, grabbing one of Augustine's mysteriously reheated french fries. "It'll be about right judgment because I think I have something to thank him for. But I think it might be time to give him a little polite advice about a bad habit!"

"I thought we had some-thing else planned for that," stammered Mark.

"The other idea did sound more exciting," admitted Melissa. "But, this might be better."

"I'll try a letter too," agreed Mark. "Grandpa, would you help us?"

'It might be time to give him a little polite advice.'

"I'd be proud to," answered Jack Foster, winking at Augustine.

"Whew! Time to go," Augustine said, standing up and stretching his tall frame. He seemed to be feeling his belly for evidence of a double chocolate soda.

"Hope you didn't make the wrong choice, Mr. Augustine," Juanita teased as the group pulled on their coats.

"Time will tell, dear," Augustine said proudly.

"Yeah, time and the bathroom scale . . ." chuckled Mark. "This guy's hooked!"

[1] Matthew 7.15
[2] Mark 13.11
[3] Psalm 106.13

A Catherine of Siena

The younger children in a family must often battle for everything they get. Born in 1347, Catherine Benincasa was the youngest of thirteen living children of Giacomo and Lapa Benincasa of Siena, Italy. Ten other children had died in infancy or early childhood.

But if the "baby Benincasa" won some victories by battling, she won many others with charm. When she was very young, Catherine had wonderful light gold hair and a personality that was always sunny. At six, while walking down the street in Siena, she saw a vision of Jesus over the top of the Dominican church. She became more quiet, more prayerful. In the following year, at the tender age of seven, she promised God that she would never marry.

The Benincasas tried to interest Catherine in young men when she was twelve. But Catherine made it clear that she had no plans for marriage. She cut off her beautiful golden hair. Angered, Lapa put the girl to work as a house servant and took away her room. Catherine had no time or place for prayer until the Lord told her to find a prayer place within her soul.

At sixteen, Catherine became a member of the Third Order of St. Dominic. She therefore wore the black-and-white habit of the Dominicans but lived at home with her family. It was an unusual situation. In those times, women either married or entered convents.

Not long after that, Catherine began to care for the sick and needy in the city of Siena. And even though she had never learned to read, people from all over began to seek her advice. All of Siena had heard about Catherine Benincasa's spiritual gifts, including the gift of right judgment. Some men and women followed Catherine so closely that they were almost always in her company. At first, her family was not happy about her lifestyle, but the Benincasas learned to live with it.

Many of the people of Siena also questioned Catherine's actions. Was it proper, they asked, for a young woman to have so many male visitors? Was it right for the young holy woman to be visiting the poorest neighborhoods in the dead of night?

Catherine seldom stopped to answer these questions. But she was often answering others. Priests, statesmen, soldiers, and intellectuals wanted to know how to save their souls. They asked her to teach them to speak with God. They wanted to know how they could find peace in an Italy where even various cities were at war with one another. Out of prayer, Catherine had the answers. As the years went by, she led many to conversions and settled disputes of all kinds. She had the gift to see the right course, the holy choice.

One of the greatest dangers for the Church during Catherine's day was the exile of the popes. For over seventy years, the popes had been living not in Rome but in Avignon, France.

Clockwise: The entrance to the home of St. Catherine in Siena, the well of its inner courtyard, and a nearby street so unchanged that Catherine would still recognize it today. This modern statue of the saint at center stands near St. Peter's Basilica in Rome.

Catherine began to write to Pope Gregory XI, urging him to return. After years of coaxing and reasoning, she was successful. Finally, in 1376, the popes were back at home in Rome.

In April of 1380, Catherine died at thirty-three. After her death, the wounds of Christ's passion, the "stigmata" appeared on her body. She became a saint in 1461 and was named a Doctor of the Church in 1970.

Photos by Carol Fleming, O.P.

You Can Tell a Tree by Its Fruit *(Matthew 7.20)*

Each tree has its own fruit — good fruit and bad fruit. Fill in examples of the kind of fruits that may be found in each tree. In this case, by fruits, we mean the effects, or results, of one's actions, or behavior. An example is provided in each tree.

We don't behave the way we do for no reason. Effects have causes. Results follow actions. So, now look again at the six fruits in each tree and suggest a cause or action that resulted in the good and bad fruits. For example, a cause of trust might be honesty. A cause for distrust might be lying.

Trust

THE HEALTHY TREE
(the tree of life)

FRUIT	CAUSE OF GOOD FRUIT
Trust	

THE DECAYED TREE
(the tree of death)

Distrust

FRUIT	CAUSE OF BAD FRUIT
Distrust	

69

Steps to Discipleship

St. John tells us every spirit that acknowledges Jesus Christ . . . belongs to God, while every spirit that fails to acknowledge him does not belong to God (1 John 4.2-3). We acknowledge Jesus Christ not just in words but in our attitudes and actions too.

Look at the following two lists of "spirits." The one on the left is negative; the one on the right is positive. Rate yourself on each of the eight scales. A "5" means your attitudes and actions show spiritual maturity and that you indeed try to acknowledge Jesus Christ in your life. A "1" means you still have a long way to go. Then circle one of the scales and think of something you can do that would raise your "score."

Spirit of Deceit I try to get what I want by trickery or falseness.	**Spirit of Honesty** My word can be taken at face value, and I am sincere.
Spirit of Meanness I am pleased when someone I don't like gets punished.	**Spirit of Kindness** I wish no harm to anyone, and I help people whenever I can.
Spirit of Selfishness I think of myself first and always take care of number one.	**Spirit of Generosity** I think of others and try to put their needs ahead of mine.
Spirit of Sensuality I desire to attract others with provocative dress or looks and suggestive language.	**Spirit of Modesty** I am careful with the way I dress, behave, and speak so as not to lure others to use me.
Spirit of Envy I feel angry when others get something I want.	**Spirit of Joy** I am happy when other people benefit and have good fortune.
Spirit of Arrogance I think I am better than others and don't mind saying so.	**Spirit of Meekness** I wish for another's qualities to be appreciated.
Spirit of Insensitivity I don't let the feelings of others get in my way.	**Spirit of Consideration** In what I do or say, I think of how it will affect others.
Spirit of Impiety I don't give much thought about God, use his name loosely, and don't participate at Mass.	**Spirit of Reverence** I make a conscious effort to pray to and worship God with care and to please him.

(Each spirit pair is separated by a scale: 1 2 3 4 5)

A Young Teen's Book of Catholic Knowledge

1. **What does the gift of right judgment empower us to do?**
   With the guidance of the Holy Spirit, it helps us make decisions in obedience to the Commandments and in accordance with the Gospel.

2. **How does the gift of right judgment help when we can't decide about something?**
   It helps us to seek guidance from others — the *right* others, those who can advise us wisely.

3. **How do parents sometimes exercise the gift of right judgment?**
   Sometimes they need the Spirit's help to arrive at decisions that might not be popular with their children.

4. **How does the gift of right judgment empower the Church?**
   It strengthens the Church to discern truth from lies, or to know what is of God and what is against God.

5. **How can I tell if someone is of God or against God?**
   Jesus said we will know them by their deeds. St. John said those who are with God are open to God's Word, while those who are against God refuse to hear or follow God's Word.

6. **How are we helped in the use of right judgment?**
   The Church's Magisterium, guided by the Holy Spirit, teaches us the true meaning of what God has revealed.

7. **What is the Magisterium?**
   The Magisterium is the teaching authority of the Church, which resides in all the bishops of the Church united with the Bishop of Rome and in the Bishop of Rome alone as the authoritative head of all the bishops.

8. **What is the responsibility of the Magisterium?**
   The Magisterium, under the guidance of the Holy Spirit, is responsible for protecting, preserving, and expressing all that God teaches through Scripture and the Tradition of the Church.

9. **What did Jesus say that points out the importance of discipleship?**
   Jesus will acknowledge to the Father whoever witnesses to him before others.

10. **What are the four ways that Catholics describe the Church in the Nicene Creed?**
    It is ONE — The Church is united to Christ its head.
    It is HOLY — The Church is guided by the Holy Spirit.
    It is CATHOLIC — The Church has a universal mission to all people of all times and places, of all nations and all races. Because of the presence and guidance of the Holy Spirit, the Church, in its ministry and Faith, draws its integrity from the Apostles.
    It is APOSTOLIC — The Church was first built on and continues to rely on the teaching and witness of the Apostles.

Chapter 7

The Powerful Gift of Knowledge

Heart Attack!

Mark was sitting in the very chair that Grandpa Foster always sat in. Somehow, Mark had told himself, if he sat there, he could bring back Grandpa's presence. In fact, there was still a trace of Grandpa's aftershave hanging in the air in the study.

But the house was cold, quiet, empty. The trace of his grandfather's presence soon faded. Mark put his face into his hands and began to cry. His tears came so fast that he barely heard the big grandfather clock chime seven right behind him.

Exactly three hours before, Mark's father had shook him out of a deep sleep. "Grandpa's had a heart attack," Mark's father told him. The words didn't sink in right away. Mark remembered looking into his father's shadowy face trying to figure out why his father had wakened him. But then, the wailing siren of an ambulance shook the fuzziness from his head, and Mark suddenly realized what was happening.

"Can I leave you and Melissa here to take care of Sally till morning?" Dad had asked.

In a nightmare of ambulance attendants and swirling lights, Grandpa was carried away. He looked deathly white. When Mark saw his face so filled with pain, terror gripped him. Sally had started to scream. Melissa had taken her sister back to her bedroom. Was Grandpa dying? Mark wondered, but he couldn't bring himself to ask.

There was a quiet look of fear on his mother's face that Mark would never forget. But before she had walked out the door to follow the stretcher and Mark's dad, she had wrapped Mark in a tight hug. "We know that God will take care of him," she whispered to him.

It was that remark that Mark seemed to hear over and over all through the day. "We know that God will take care of him." At 7:30 A.M., Mark's mother had called to tell them that Grandpa was in intensive care. "We don't know . . ." she said when Mark asked her if Grandpa would live. Mark decided to go to school, but his parents allowed the girls to skip school and go to their aunt's house three miles away.

Mark told Jesse about Grandpa Foster's heart attack when they met in language-arts class. Jesse seemed shocked but tried to console Mark. "Hey, your grandpa is one tough guy!" Jesse assured him. Jesse seemed to have nothing else to say. "I'll pray," Jesse told his best friend finally, grasping him around the shoulder. Jesse went off to science class. Mark went off to gym class grateful to have a friend like Jesse.

Even so, Mark did little else but worry at school. At noon and again at 2:00 P.M., Mark called the hospital to ask about John Foster. There was nothing new to learn. Mark decided to walk to St. Ignatius rectory from school. He would see if Father Mike could say a special Mass for his grandfather's recovery right away.

A Vigil of Prayer for Grandpa Foster

At 5:15 P.M. the next day, Father Mike Rogers was celebrating a special Mass for the recovery of John Foster. At 3:00 P.M., Melissa and Mark walked the four blocks to Sally's school to pick her up. They all planned to spend an hour at the library before walking to St. Ignatius for the Mass. Later, they were to take the city bus to their aunt's house. Their parents were still spending every available moment at the hospital. It was "touch and go." They had gone to Mass earlier in the day "for Grandpa."

The late-afternoon sun was pouring through the stained-glass windows on the west side of old St. Ignatius. Mark, Melissa, and Sally left their schoolbooks on top of the broken radi-

ator and made their way up the aisle. Father Mike came out of the sacristy, nodded warmly at them, and began the Mass.

At the handshake of peace, Mark and Melissa turned around to find their friends Jesse and Juanita in the pew behind them. Mark just "knew" that Augustine would be there too. There, on the other side of the church, next to one of the pillars, was the tall figure of Augustine. Suddenly, Mark realized how he had missed talking to Augustine during this crisis.

"Peace be with you all," Augustine smiled. He had walked across the center aisle to reach out for the McIntyres. With his hand inside the big, strong grip of Augustine, Mark now felt a peace, if only a small peace, about Grandpa.

"May I take all of you young people home?" Augustine asked.

Augustine was in the vestibule waiting for the McIntyres and their friends when Mass was over. Dressed in a bright blue raincoat, he also had an umbrella tucked under his arm.

"Thanks for the offer," said Mark, picking up his books and Sally's from the long dead radiator. "We were going to take the bus," he told Augustine, "but if it wouldn't be too far out of your way...."

"Yeah, thanks, I'd like that," agreed Juanita. "Me too," added Jesse.

"Did you know about our grandfather's heart attack?" Melissa asked Augustine. The five had piled into the red car Augustine was warming up. Melissa had Sally on her lap, and Mark's left knee was wedged against her. Juanita was on her other side trying to hang onto a stack of schoolbooks.

"Yes, Melissa, I did," replied Augustine softly.

"I thought you would," Melissa replied. Deeply frightened about her grandfather, Melissa had not said more than four words since the day before. "You probably know how he is right now, then don't you," continued Melissa. "You probably even know if he is going to die!"

Melissa's voice now betrayed her fear, her sense of helplessness. Sally began to whimper but pushed her face into Melissa's coat.

"Melissa," Augustine said gently, "only the Lord knows our futures. That wasn't the kind of knowledge he wanted any of us to have. Do you remember what he even told his Apostles, his best friends? He said: 'Stay awake, therefore! You cannot know the day your Lord is coming.'[1]

"But, there is a special knowledge that the Lord does give," Augustine insisted. Sally was still crying a bit, but otherwise the car was much too quiet. "Let's stop here at the park for one minute, and I can show you something about it."

We Walk by Faith, Not by Sight

Augustine pulled into the drive to Memorial Park near the picnic tables. The daylight was going, but a handsome splash of orange and pink still painted the western sky through the trees. Augustine climbed up to sit on top of the picnic table and lifted Sally up onto his lap. Mark and Jesse sat on the ground, their backs up against a huge oak. Melissa stood eyeing Augustine carefully. She looked as if she were ready to move away at a moment's notice. Juanita sat down on the bench with a view of the sunset.

But for a minute or two, Augustine said nothing. Finally, high above them, a turtledove began to coo. Then, a second one began the same mournful song.

Augustine's face lit up in a smile, and he squeezed Sally.

"That's it!" Augustine laughed. "That's a dove! But did you know that turtledoves are also sometimes called 'rain crows'? God tells them and the rest of the animal kingdom how to know when it is going to rain."

Jesse looked at Mark as though Augustine had finally gone off the deep end, and Augustine caught the look. Melissa's expression hadn't changed. She still stood straight up, studying this man with her arms folded firmly in front of her. She was waiting. "Show me!" was written all over her.

"Look," Augustine said. "You all saw that I wore a raincoat and carried an umbrella tonight. That's because I listened to a late forecast on the radio. But these birds and animals of the park have this knowledge about rain, storms, and cold winters inside them." Augustine shifted Sally to his knee and tapped his chest symbolically. "The Father who created them gives them a knowledge that is not like the knowledge I got from switching on WXRY!"

But these lessons were quickly beyond Sally's in-

terest. She hopped down and began to pick up acorns and put them in her coat pocket.

"God also gives us a great gift of knowledge," continued Augustine. "When you are confirmed, this gift will be recharged and renewed in you. It is one of the seven gifts of the Holy Spirit, another gift of power, or grace."

"Well, that'll be good for Jesse," laughed Juanita. "His mom says he never has had any sense about the weather."

"Ha!" laughed Augustine. "I'm afraid that you may not be headed for any improvement there, Jesse. God's gift of knowledge works in areas that are much more important than knowing when it will rain. This knowledge gives a deep trust and sureness about the Lord, about what God has told us. Because of it, we can live with a kind of confidence and focus that wouldn't be possible otherwise. This gift of knowledge strengthens faith, helps us to see beyond the wisdom of the world. It assures us that God will provide and that we need not cling possessively to the things of the world."

Just then, the dove cooed again, high beyond the picnic table where one man and five young people rested and watched the daylight dying.

"Your grandfather knows that the Lord is watching over him," Augustine said, smiling. "He knows the Lord as surely as that turtle-dove knows about the rain." Melissa looked at Augustine as though she were just beginning to understand the day's math problems. "Don't worry," pleaded Augustine, looking first at Mark, then at Melissa. "His Father will take care of him no matter what, and I believe he knows it."

"What do you mean 'no matter what'?" Melissa asked suspiciously. "You said that the Lord is watching over him."

"He is, Melissa," Augustine again reassured her. "Even if the Lord were to take your grandfather now, remember that death is not the end for those who believe in Jesus as Lord and Savior. When we die in God's grace, or love, death ushers us into eternal life. It's like a 'happy birthday to eternity.' Your grandfather knows that, too, and that is why he's not afraid."

Dark spots had begun to plop upon the green wooden picnic table. "Oh, it's raining," called Sally. She stuffed two more acorns into bulging pockets and ran to Melissa. In two minutes, Augustine's red car was again buzzing down the street. The rain had become a downpour in just a few minutes.

Help My Lack of Trust

"Mr. Augustine," began Mark, "what if someone's faith is really weak? Will the gift of knowledge do anything for a faith like that?" The car had stopped for a red light. Against the regular swish of windshield wipers back and forth on the window, Mark's question sounded very urgent.

"Let me answer with a story," Augustine said, putting the car into gear again as the light changed. "It begins with a father who is really worried about his son. The son, you see, had an illness that no one had been able to get under control. The boy would have seizures and would foam at the mouth. The father was desperate, because he thought the illness would kill his son.

"This father came to Jesus. He said to the Lord: 'If out of the kindness of your heart you can do anything to help us, please do!' 'If you can?' Jesus said to him. 'Everything is possible to a man who trusts.' Right there, the father understood how weak his faith was. But he accepted himself where

he was. The man told Jesus: 'I do believe! Help my lack of trust.'[2] Then Jesus healed the boy and gave him back to his father in perfect health. Don't you think that father and son knew God in a deeper way after that?"

Augustine had stopped at Juanita's house, and Jesse borrowed the umbrella to take her to the door through the pouring rain. "Whew!" exclaimed Jesse as he hopped back into the car. "That turtledove at the park really did know something about the rain!" As Jesse got out at his house, Mark ran him to the front door and then came back with the big, wet umbrella.

'Death is not the end for those who believe in Jesus.'

At exatly 6:00 P.M., the little red car pulled into a driveway on Claremont Street. The front porch light was on, and a woman was standing at the window peering out. Augustine got out, opened up the large umbrella, and then helped the girls to the front door.

"Thank you so much for giving the children a ride," smiled Aunt Margie, shaking Augustine's hand. "They did so want to go to

Mass this afternoon, but I had no car to pick them up."

"My pleasure," grinned Augustine, winking at Sally staring at him from the hallway.

"I have good news!" exclaimed Aunt Margie. The door was barely shut against the rain and wind.

Mark wheeled around from the closet where he was hanging up Sally's coat. "What is it? Is it about Grandpa?"

"Yes!" responded Aunt Margie, grinning from ear to ear. "Your parents called about an hour ago. Your grandpa came out of the coma and said to them, 'I know it's gonna rain. I know it's gonna rain.' This was even before it had started to thunder and rain. They knew he was just babbling, but the doctors see it as a good sign."

"I knew it!" yelled Melissa, heaving her hat up against the ceiling.

"Sure you did, sis!" Mark grinned, shaking his head. But he felt generous, brotherly. He reached out and grabbed his one and only twin and gave her a hug. Not wanting to be left out, Sally grabbed Aunt Margie around the waist and started to giggle.

[1] Matthew 24.42.
[2] Mark 9.22-24.

A Young Teen's Book of Catholic Knowledge

1. **What power does the gift of knowledge give us?**
   It instructs us about God and gives us a deep trust and sureness about him.

2. **How does trust in the Lord affect our lives?**
   It provides moorings for our lives and helps us to live with a confidence that is founded in the unfailing love of God.

3. **How does the gift of knowledge help us relate to possessions?**
   It assures us that God will provide and that we need not cling possessively to things.

4. **What should a person do when he realizes his faith is weak?**
   He should ask the Lord for strength with a prayer like the one found in Scripture: "I do believe! Help my lack of trust" (Mark 9.24).

5. **What are some things that get in the way of believing fully in the Faith?**
   Ignorance of the truths of the Faith; inability to accept the truths of Faith as really true; unwillingness to believe because of laziness, disinterest, or because of the changes that would need to be made in our lives as a result of belief.

6. **How did Jesus respond to the Apostle Thomas's initial disbelief in the risen Jesus?**
   He said that Thomas became a believer because he saw him (Jesus), but those who have not seen him and believed are blessed.

7. **How does the gift of knowledge help us to believe in the truths of the Faith?**
   It helps us to hold fast to truth, to avoid doubt, and to evaluate all things according to the truths of Scripture and the teachings of the Church.

8. **What are the most basic beliefs of Christians concerning God, the Father?**
   Christians believe that he is Almighty and that he is the Creator of heaven and earth.

9. **What are the most basic beliefs of Christians concerning the risen Jesus?**
   Jesus is our Lord, the Messiah or Savior, the Son of the living God, who rose from the dead and sits at the right hand of the Father and will come to judge the living and the dead.

10. **What do Christians basically believe about Jesus as man?**
    He was conceived by the Holy Spirit, born of a woman, the Virgin Mary, and suffered, was crucified, and died for our sins.

11. **In addition to the Father and Jesus Christ, what are the other most basic beliefs of Christians?**
    Christians believe in the Holy Spirit, the holy catholic Church, the communion of saints, the forgiveness of sins, the resurrection of the body, and life everlasting.

St. Thomas Aquinas

The seventh son of a nobleman and his wife, Thomas was born in Roccasecca near Cassino, Italy, in 1225. His parents were wealthy and could afford to send their sons to the best schools. Count Landulf of Aquino hoped that his sons had good minds, but he began to see that his little Thomas was the most capable of them all.

At the early age of five, the little boy was enrolled in a school at the nearby

A likeness of St. Thomas greets visitors to the church of Fossanova near Naples, where St. Thomas died.

Photo by Ca Flemi O.P.

Benedictine abbey at Monte Cassino. The long and wonderful road of learning began. Thomas was a keen student of all kinds of learning, but one subject, above all, was his favorite. That was the study of God. Often during his free moments, the young son of Count Landulf thought about his favorite mystery. "What is God?" "What is God like?" He turned the questions over and over in his mind.

At fourteen, Thomas was growing up. He was to be a big man — six feet, six inches tall. But he was also "outgrowing" his school at Monte Casino. He was sent to Naples, Italy, to study. Thomas was very quiet in class. He was so quiet that the other students thought he was stupid. Because of this and because of his size, he got the nickname "the dumb ox."

But nothing was further from the truth! Inside this quiet young man was the best mind the Church was to see for many centuries. His desire was to spend his life learning and teaching about God. At Naples, he had a wonderful teacher who was a Dominican. Though Thomas was from a noble family, he decided to join these Dominicans, who often supported themselves by begging.

When his parents heard that Thomas planned to become a Dominican and not a Benedictine, they were upset. His Dominican superiors thought Thomas should study in Paris until the family calmed down. But on the road to Paris, two of his brothers stopped Thomas and kidnapped him. He was a prisoner in his own home for more than a year.

Under lock and key, Thomas followed the Dominican rules and prayers. His sister and mother were impressed with the faithful prayer of Thomas. One day, his mother kissed him good-bye and helped him to escape. He was off to the Dominicans again.

Thomas then studied the work of the ancient Greek philosopher Aristotle. Aristotle, of course, had been a pagan. But fifteen hundred years later, his thinking still touched every area of study. Thomas brilliantly used the thought of Aristotle to explain the teaching of the Church. Better than anyone else in his day, Thomas presented his explanation of this teaching in a long work that he called the *Summa Theologiae* or "Summary of Theology," one of the most influential theological works ever written.

But if Thomas had a great mind, he may have had an even greater gift for prayer. In the end, more real knowledge came through prayer. Each day, he would kneel in prayer for hours. Then, he would get up, sit at his desk and write. He was learning what to write during prayer!

One day while saying Mass in 1273, a great look of joy and surprise came upon him. Later, he told his assistant that he would write no more for the *Summa.* He had received some great new knowledge, realized a new truth that he could not explain. God was teaching Thomas in a way that books could never do.

"In comparison to the things I have seen, and that have been revealed to me, everything I have written seems [like] straw," Thomas explained.

Thomas had also come to know that his death was near. In 1274, he became ill while on a journey. He died at the age of forty-nine and was named a saint less than 50 years later. Later still, he was named a Doctor of the Church and patron saint of schools.

Steps to Discipleship

The Apostles' Creed is a statement of the fundamental beliefs of Christians. It reflects the teachings of the Apostles, although it is believed to have originated in the second century. Today it is most commonly used at Baptism and as the first prayer in reciting of the Rosary. The gift of knowledge gives us the power to hold fast to these Christian truths.

Take each of the following statements from the Apostles' Creed and look up the Scripture passage that explains or applies to the statement. Fill in the missing words.

I believe

"We have that spirit of faith of which the Scripture says, 'Because I believed, I _____ _____ .' We believe and so we speak, knowing that he who raised up the Lord Jesus will raise us up along with Jesus. . ." (2 Corinthians 4.13-14).

in God,

"They claim to 'know God,' but by their _____ they _____ that he exists" (Titus 1.16).

the Father almighty,

"Bow _____ under God's mighty hand, so that in due time he may

_____ you high" (1 Peter 5.6).

Creator of heaven and earth;

"Everything God created is _____; nothing is to be rejected when it is received with thanksgiving. . ." (1 Timothy 4.4).

and in Jesus Christ, his only Son,

"Yes, God so loved the world that he gave his only Son, that whoever

_____ _____ _____ may not die but may have

_____ _____ ." (John 3.16).

our Lord,

"For if you _____ with your lips that Jesus is Lord, and

_____ in your heart that God raised him from the dead, you will be saved" (Romans 10.9).

who was conceived by the Holy Spirit,

"They were _____ with the Holy Spirit and continued to speak God's

word with_____" (Acts 4.31).

born of the Virgin Mary,

"Rather, he _____ himself and took the form of a slave, being born

in the _____ of men" (Philippians 2.7).

suffered under Pontius Pilate,

"Christ suffered in the flesh; therefore, arm yourselves with his same mentality. He who has suffered in the flesh has

_____ _____ _____.

You are not to spend what remains of your

earthly life on_____

_____ but on the will of God" (1 Peter 4.1-2).

was crucified, died, and was buried.

"It was through the law that I died to the law, to live for God. I have been crucified with Christ, and the life I live now is

not my own; _____

_____ _____ _____ _____ ." (Galatians 2.19 20).

80

He descended into hell;

"Now, since the children are men of blood and flesh, Jesus likewise had a full share in ours, that by his death he might

_____ _____ _____ ,

the prince of death, of his power, and

_____ _____ who through fear of death had been slaves their whole life long" (Hebrews 2.14-15).

the third day he rose again from the dead.

"Now has judgment come upon this world, now will this world's prince be driven out, and I — once I am lifted up from earth —

will_____ all men to myself" (John 12.31-32).

He ascended into heaven and sits at the right hand of God, the Father almighty;

"In my Father's house there are many dwelling places; otherwise, how could I have told you that I was going to prepare a place for you? I am

indeed going to_____

__ _____ _____ _____ ,

and then I shall come back to take you with me, that where I am you also may be" (John 14.2-3).

from thence he shall come to judge the living and the dead.

"He commissioned us to preach to the people

and to bear witness that he is the one_____

_____ _____ _____ as judge of the living and the dead" (Acts 10.42).

I believe in the Holy Spirit,

"The Spirit we have received is not the world's spirit but God's Spirit, helping us to

_____ _____

_____ he has given us" (1 Corinthians 2.12).

the holy catholic Church,

"You are strangers and aliens no longer. No, you

are_____ _____ of the saints and members of the household of God. You form a building which rises on the foundation of the apostles and prophets, with Christ Jesus himself as the capstone. Through him the whole structure is fitted together and takes

shape as a_____

_____ in the Lord; in him you are being built into this temple, to become a dwelling place for God in the Spirit" (Ephesians 2.19-22).

the communion of saints,

"God has so constructed the body as to give greater honor to the lowly members, that there may be no dissension in the body, but that all the members may be

_____ for one another. If one member suffers, all the members suffer with it; if one member is honored, all the members share its joy" (1 Corinthians 12.24-26).

the forgiveness of sins,

"Forgive us the wrong _____ have done as we forgive those who wrong us" (Matthew 6.12).

the resurrection of the body,

"Do not, therefore, let sin rule your mortal body and make you obey its lusts; no more shall you offer the members of your body to sin as weapons for evil. Rather, offer yourselves to God as men who have come back from the dead to

life, and your_____ to God as weapons for justice" (Romans 6.12-13).

and the life everlasting.

"Eternal life is this: to know you, the only true God, and him whom you have

sent, _____ _____"
(John 17.3).

Chapter 8

The Powerful Gift of Understanding

Why Does God Permit Bad Things to Happen?

"I just don't understand," Juanita cried with anguish. "Look at this, Mom!"

The Sunday paper was spread out on the kitchen table. It was filled with pictures of the earthquake in Mexico. The quake had killed thousands. Juanita and her mother were very worried about her uncle, her mother's younger brother. Father Pedro was studying in Mexico City.

Somehow, Juanita felt sure that her uncle Pedro was safe. But these children, these babies! Staring at her from the front page was a picture of a baby about nine months old. She was sitting in the rubble of a house where her parents and brothers had all died. She was crying, with one small fist rubbing tears away from her right eye. She looked so frightened.

"Mother," Juanita said, staring at the picture, "I don't understand how God lets this happen. Look!"

But Mrs. Sanchez wasn't in the kitchen. Often, Juanita noticed, her mother would now pray in her bedroom after meals. Ever since Clara Sanchez had started to attend the parish prayer meetings, Juanita had seen a change in her.

"Why?" Juanita asked herself. She reached for the kitchen scissors and cut out the picture of the crying baby. Juanita took it to her room and pinned it up on her bulletin board.

Later that afternoon, a priest in Father Pedro's order called her mother. Father Pedro was safe, he said. Juanita was relieved. But when her mother started to cry after hanging up the phone, Juanita realized how frightened her mother had been. And yet, in Juanita there was a leftover sadness. She was struggling to understand why things like earthquakes hurt innocent people. Wasn't God watching over everyone?

After school on Monday afternoon, Juanita, Jesse, and the twins headed for the public library. In social-studies class, they had been given a research project to do. Because of the earthquake, their teacher asked them to investigate other disasters in history and find out how different peoples handled them.

Mark and Jesse had jogged ahead of Juanita and Melissa to get "the best books." But as she walked along with Melissa, Juanita wondered if she'd really find the answers. Her "bulletin-board baby" kept coming to mind.

"What ails ya, Sanchez?" Melissa asked finally. "You haven't said a word since we left school."

"Oh, not much," Juanita answered quietly. "Maybe Augustine can help me understand." Juanita mumbled to herself.

"Say what?" Melissa said, opening the library door.

"I was just thinking," Juanita said, "that maybe Augustine could help me understand how these natural disasters happen."

"Sure he can," giggled Melissa. "He was an antique when Moses was still in diapers!"

"Shame on you, Melissa!" laughed a shocked Juanita.

"Shhhhhhhhhhh," came a warning from an older woman at the library desk.

The girls headed for the card catalog where Mark and Jesse were already busy. They soon got busy too. At 4:00 P.M., Augustine was meeting them in one of the conference rooms.

A Special Meeting in the Library

Forty-five minutes later, all four were gathered with Augustine in a conference room in the library basement. There was a bit more to say about Confirmation, Augustine told them. They were to receive the sacrament in just a few weeks. Augustine had apparently been doing some yard work. He had on an old green jacket, they noticed. He hadn't done much physical work in his "life before," Augustine once informed them. Now he loved it!

"I want to make sure that you have a full understanding of Confirmation," remarked Augustine, leaning back in one of the library chairs. "And that, by the way, is the subject today."

"What is?" asked Jesse, looking bewildered.

"I just told you," responded Augustine.

"I don't understand either," added Mark.

"But that's it!" laughed Augustine.

"*Not understanding* is the subject?" piped up Melissa scratching her head.

"That and understanding. The gift of understanding!" Augustine grinned. "I just wanted to see if you were paying attention after a long day at school. And it looks as if you have work to do tonight." Augustine was staring at the small stack of books they each had.

"We're studying natural disasters," explained Juanita. "We have to find out how people have coped with them in the past."

"Ah, I see," said Augustine, nodding his head. "There's a lot to learn there. I like to think of the way Job coped with disasters. Do you remember his story?"

'They are in God's time. He takes care of them now.'

"Didn't he get sick and lose his money?" Mark asked.

"Yes," agreed Augustine, "and much more than money. Job's ten children were also killed. Then, all of his livestock died, and all of his friends abandoned him. Even Job's wife began to believe that God was punishing Job for some great sin."

"Well, wasn't he?" asked Juanita.

"No," explained Augustine, "but God was testing him. Job disappointed the devil, who wanted Job to get angry at God. But Job just kept believing that God would take care of him in the end. Job *never understood* why these things happened, but he believed that God had a plan."

"What are we supposed to think about all those Mexican people killed," demanded Juanita. "I have a picture of a little baby whose whole family was killed. Now she's an orphan!" There was anger in her voice and just a hint of tears in the girl's dark eyes.

"It's a great loss," said Augustine gently, looking at Juanita. "But remember, those who were lost to their families and friends in Mexico are only lost to our time. Now they are in God's time. He takes care of them now. He sets everything right in his own time. You must believe that, Juanita."

"It's hard," mumbled Juanita, looking down.

"I know," agreed Augustine, knowing the pain in her heart.

"But remember the pain and suffering that Jesus went through. His enemies plotted against him. Judas betrayed him. He was accused and tried falsely. He was flogged and finally nailed to a cross."

"Those were terrible things," Juanita cried out, "but what have they got to do with the people who died in the earthquake?"

"Well, look at it this way," Augustine said. "When Jesus suffered and died on the cross out of love for us, he changed the meaning of all those terrible, evil things in the world.

"For us who try to walk with God, Jesus is our strength and comfort in the face of every evil. Remember what I told you once before: You can now even be glad to share in the sufferings of Christ, because when he comes, you will be filled with joy. It wasn't like that before Jesus died on the cross. The world has always had suffering, but Christ is the one who made it mean something. The world has always had death, but Christ turned it into a gateway to eternal life. That's why we say Jesus overcame evil and death."

Augustine knew how difficult these great mysteries were, and admired the patience of his young friends. "It will take time," said Augustine, "but with the gift of understanding, you will be-

gin to grasp these mysteries with your own heart."

Value the Things That Matter

"The gift of understanding," Augustine continued, "is one of the seven gifts of the Holy Spirit, as you know. Understanding helps us to see the Lord and his ways more deeply. Jesus once told his disciples to watch out for the teaching of the Pharisees and Sadducees, but the disciples missed the point completely. Jesus responded: 'How weak your faith is! Do you still not understand?'[1]

So, now do you see what the key to understanding is?" asked Augustine.

"Faith, right?" Jesse answered.

"Yeah," Mark added.

"And you need to be open to the Spirit working through you, just like with the other gifts."

"Good," Augustine responded with a smile. "The gift of understanding is not something that belongs to the educated. It is a spiritual thing. It belongs to those who trust in the Lord and listen to the Spirit. As St. Paul said, when our love is full of understanding, we 'learn to value the things that really matter.'[2] For

those who trust, understanding adds power and depth to prayer life. It also strengthens our appreciation of the sacraments. And it empowers us with a deeper sense of the meaning of Scripture. Ask your mother about that, Juanita."

"My mother?" Juanita said with surprise. She didn't know that Augustine had ever talked with her mother since the party.

Augustine leaned back in

the chair until it rested against the wall. The conference room seemed to cramp the style of this tall man who still claimed to be older than any book in the library upstairs.

"This gift of understanding," said Augustine, "strengthens our faith. It helps our minds to have some knowledge of God's truths even when things happen that make no sense — like earthquakes, floods, fires, droughts, sudden death, accidents! When we see these things with the gift of understanding, we can persevere the way Job did in the Old Testament."

Just then, someone was rapping sharply on the large glass window that looked out into the basement hallway. Augustine turned his head as if to see who would dare interrupt a Doctor of the Church.

There, peeking through partly closed curtains, was the library's senior librarian, Miss Smootley. She had fire in her eyes and was pointing vigorously toward a sign on the wall.

"Please treat all library furniture with care!" The words were printed in bold red type. The librarian then stared at Augustine who was still leaning back in his chair against the wall.

"Oh, forgive me!" Augus-

tine seemed to pray. He leaned forward, and the front legs of his chair smacked down hard. Seeing that order was restored, Miss Smootley disappeared.

"Close that drape, will you Jesse?" Augustine said, wiping his brow. But for a minute, Jesse could do nothing. All four students were rolling with laughter, but Augustine quickly regained his dignity.

"Think of this gift of understanding as a key," Augustine said leaning forward now, elbows on the table. "It helps us open the door to deeper faith. Jesus believed that this understanding was very important. He too saw it as a power to 'unlock' greater truths.

" 'Are you, too, incapable of understanding?'[3] Jesus asked his Apostles when they wanted to know what a certain parable meant," Augustine said. "He wanted them to see deeper, to enter that richer kingdom of faith with the key of understanding."

It was getting late. Within a few minutes, the four gathered their books and put on their jackets. Juanita also picked up an envelope of materials that Augustine was sending to her mother. They said their good-byes to Augustine.

"Oh, by the way Mr. Augustine, if you use that library exit over there," Mark added, pointing across the room, "you won't have to pass Miss Smootley's desk."

A Different Kind of Gift

It was five when the twins and Juanita stopped in front of Juanita's house, where her mother was already home from work. Inside, Juanita found her mother in the kitchen with the Bible in front of her. The spicy aroma of spaghetti sauce filled the kitchen.

"I have something for you from Mr. Augustine," Juanita said after leaning down to kiss her mother "hello." Then Juanita watched as her mother poured the contents of the envelope out on the table. She acted as though she were opening a present.

"I really wanted more things to read about Scripture," explained Clara Sanchez, looking up a bit shyly at her only child. "Honey, something is really opening my eyes," she said. "It's exciting." Juanita said nothing but unzipped her jacket and sat down. Her mother usually talked only about what was on sale, how the "Cubbies" were doing, or "family matters."

"I became more in-terested in all this when you started to study for Confirmation," Clara Sanchez smiled. "I wanted to know more about the Holy Spirit so I could help you. But when I went to the prayer meeting, I got interested for my own sake too."

"Juanita," her mother said with excitement, "in one of his letters to the Christians at Corinth, St. Paul tells about the spiritual gifts that Christians first received when the Church was very young. They received special gifts of wisdom, knowledge, faith, healing, prophecy, tongues, and the gift of explaining what the tongue, or language, meant. I'd never even heard about that!" Clara Sanchez said. "But now I can see that some of this is happening to Christians today. All these things were given to strengthen Christians."

Juanita loved her mother dearly, but some of this sounded a little unbelievable. Her mother saw the doubtful look in her daughter's face. Mrs. Sanchez stopped talking and finished preparing dinner. The smell of the spaghetti sauce was making Juanita's mouth water. A little later, they sat down to eat.

"Mom," said Juanita with her mouth a bit full. "Did you get any of these gifts?"

Clara Sanchez put down her forkful of spaghetti. A strange smile came across her face. "Yes," she said finally. "I began to speak in a tongue, a different language. It was like feeling so overwhelmed by God's love, that these words just poured out like a prayer of thanksgiving."

"I understand . . ." said Juanita quietly, smiling back at her mother.

Juanita had never known her mother to "stretch the truth." She thought for a moment of her "bulletin-board baby." She didn't really understand why God did the things he did. Earthquakes and tongues and mothers who made such spaghetti! The world was full of terrible and wonderful mysteries. God understood how and why they all came to be. Maybe, she told herself, remembering *that* was what the gift of understanding really meant.

"Is there any more spaghetti?" Juanita asked a moment later.

---

1 Matthew 16.8-9.
2 Philippians 1.10.
3 Mark 7.18.

A Young Teen's Book of Catholic Knowledge

1. **What does the gift of understanding do?**
   It empowers us to see the Lord and his ways more deeply.

2. **Is the gift of understanding given only to the highly educated?**
   No, it is given to those who trust in the Lord and who listen to the Spirit.

3. **How does the gift of understanding affect the way we live our faith?**
   It adds power and depth to our prayer. It deepens our appreciation of the sacraments. It also gives us a deeper sense of the meaning of Scripture.

4. **What can we do to receive the gift of understanding?**
   We need to be open to the Spirit and let the Spirit's power work through us.

5. **How can I be an understanding person?**
   By developing such qualities as acceptance, open-mindedness, and sensitivity to others.

6. **What are the different types of gifts from God?**
   God freely gives people many different types of gifts. In the broadest sense, life itself is a gift from God. God also gives each person many natural gifts, or talents and abilities. In addition, God gives each person many spiritual gifts.

7. **What kinds of spiritual gifts does God give?**
   The Church and the Seven Sacraments are gifts from God. In addition, there are spiritual gifts, called charisms, or charismatic gifts. Charisms are gifts to be used in the service of others.

8. **What is the purpose of the spiritual gifts, or charisms?**
   The gifts of the Holy Spirit are given for the renewal and upbuilding of the Church.

9. **What does it mean that we should no longer live as the pagans do, with minds empty and understanding darkened?**
   We should not live like those who reject or ignore God. We must learn to value the things that really matter.

10. **What does it mean that we should acquire a fresh, spiritual way of thinking?**
    We should base our lives on God's law and love, and desire to please him.

St. Bernadette

More than a million pilgrims visit Lourdes each year to seek the healing waters that began to flow when Bernadette dug with her hands at the spot pointed out to her by Our Lady.

NC Photo

Though she was never taller than four feet, eight inches, she was the eldest child, and she acted like it. In southern France, being born first meant something. Born in a little village in the Pyrenées mountains in 1844 to François and Louise Soubirous, Bernadette, even though she was a girl, was the family heir. As such, she had authority and responsibility.

But Bernadette must have wondered what her authority was really worth that day in 1858. It was February 11th. To gather firewood for the noonday cooking, she walked out of town with her sister Toinette and her cousin Jeanne.

At fourteen, Bernadette suffered badly from asthma and couldn't go fast. So, the other two ran ahead all the same. They also refused to carry her across the stream where they had stripped off shoes and stockings to cross. Bernadette knew that getting her feet wet would make her asthma cough worse, but there seemed to be no other way.

"I had just removed the first stocking when I heard a noise something like a gust of wind," she explained later.

Bernadette looked all around at trees that were still. Glancing back toward a rock grotto, she saw something. It was a young woman glowing with light and dressed in a white gown with a blue sash. Only later did she come to understand that it was the Blessed Virgin Mary.

This was the first of a series of eighteen apparitions to Bernadette. She had always been a good girl who said her prayers. But visions of the Blessed Virgin Mary? At first, her mother didn't believe her, and neither did most of Lourdes.

Several months later, the apparitions had stopped but something else had begun. People who washed in the spring that had begun to flow near the grotto were being healed of all kinds of illnesses. Soon, all of France knew of Lourdes and the healing waters of the spring. Bernadette became a "celebrity."

Within a few years, Bernadette knew what she wanted. She wanted to enter religious life, but her poor health was a problem. At twenty-two, she finally boarded a train for Nevers, France. There, she entered the convent of the Sisters of Charity and never returned to Lourdes.

Even in the convent, people tried to touch or talk with the young woman who had talked with the Blessed Virgin. Bernadette understood very well that she did not deserve special treatment. She tried hard to avoid curious visitors — even bishops! But the little nun wished to be, as she said, put behind the door like a broom after use.

In her own quiet ways, Bernadette had become very close to God. But Bernadette's was a very simple sort of holiness. After the apparitions, she had learned to read. She didn't get much schooling, but she loved to read the Bible, especially the Passion of Jesus. And when she was in prayer, others sometimes watched her. That wonderful glow of happiness came upon her. They knew that Bernadette was thinking of "her" Virgin and praying to the Virgin's Son.

"I do not promise to make you happy in this world, but in the next." That's what Our Lady of Lourdes had told Bernadette during one of the apparitions. Bernadette grew to understand the meaning of this prediction. She suffered greatly from almost constant sickness due to asthma. But the girl from Lourdes also grew to understand what faith and charity were all about. With great humility, she served the Lord and then died after a long and painful illness in 1879. She was thirty-five years old. In 1933, she became a canonized saint.

What Are My Natural Gifts?

When we speak of gifts, there are many types. We have thus far dealt with six of the *seven gifts of the Holy Spirit.* They give us power — the power, or grace, of the Holy Spirit acting through us. These seven gifts are given to all in Baptism and are strengthened in the Sacrament of Confirmation.

There are also, however, *natural gifts,* or *talents,* that God has given each of us for various tasks in life. As with all of God's gifts, they should be used for the glorification of God and in service to our brothers and sisters.

Below you will find two lists: Service to the Community *and* Service to the Parish. *They reflect some of the many service roles in which Catholic Christians live out their faith. Some of the natural gifts that are needed for those roles are listed as well. As you consider each role, first ask yourself the following question and then mark your answer.*

**Do I have, or would I like to have
the gifts, or talents, for this role?**

SERVICE TO THE COMMUNITY

One Who Provides Food and Clothing for the Hungry and Poor
— conducts or contributes to food banks, food pantries, "meals on wheels," Thanksgiving clothing drives, etc. The *GIFTS* needed: a caring personality, sensitivity to good diet, organizer, missionary zeal against hunger.

　　　　MY RESPONSE: YES ＿＿ MAYBE ＿＿ NO ＿＿

Ministry to the Elderly — provides companionship and assistance to the elderly in retirement homes or to those who live alone in their own homes. The *GIFTS* needed: a caring personality, sensitivity to the elderly, patience, gentleness.

　　　　MY RESPONSE: YES ＿＿ MAYBE ＿＿ NO ＿＿

Ministry to the Physically or Mentally Disabled — assists the disabled to find employment, assists in special olympics or other similar activities, and acts as a helper when trips are organized for these persons. The *GIFTS* needed: a caring personality, sensitivity to the disabled, patience, and persistence.

　　　　MY RESPONSE: ＿＿ MAYBE ＿＿ NO ＿＿

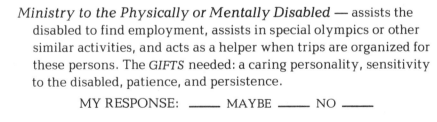

Pro-life Ministry — opposes abortion through educational and legislative activities, provides help and encouragement to women with unwanted pregnancies, provides assistance to unwed mothers. The *GIFTS* needed: the courage of one's conviction, compassion, persistence.

　　　　MY RESPONSE: YES ＿＿ MAYBE ＿＿ NO ＿＿

SERVICE TO THE PARISH

Catechist — teaches religious education or CCD. The *GIFTS* needed: faith, talent for teaching, and the ability to enjoy children.

    MY RESPONSE: YES _____ MAYBE _____ NO _____

Parish Council Member — elected or appointed to help the pastor keep the parish growing and active. The *GIFTS* needed: a talent for planning and organizing. It also helps to be a person with ideas and vision.

    MY RESPONSE: YES _____ MAYBE _____ NO _____

Finance Committee Member or Fund Raiser — makes budgets and establishes a balance between projects and funds available. The *GIFTS* needed: skill at budgeting, imagination, and a taste for hard work.

    MY RESPONSE: YES _____ MAYBE _____ NO _____

Building and Maintenance Committee Member — plans and carries out new construction to meet parish needs, and keeps up repair of parish buildings and grounds. The *GIFTS* needed: the ability to organize, as well as mechanical and building skills.

    MY RESPONSE: YES _____ MAYBE _____ NO _____

Singer in Choir or Folk Group — (self explanatory). The *GIFTS* needed: a good voice or musical skill and dependability.

    MY RESPONSE: _____ MAYBE _____ NO _____

Lector — proclaims the Scripture readings at Mass. The *GIFTS* needed: a love for God's Word, a talent for public reading, and an easy-to-hear voice.

    MY RESPONSE: YES _____ MAYBE _____ NO _____

Eucharistic Minister — helps distribute Communion at Mass or to the sick or homebound. The *GIFTS* needed: a deep devotion to the Eucharist. It also helps to have a dignified manner.

    MY RESPONSE: YES _____ MAYBE _____ NO _____

Greeter/Usher — welcomes people as they assemble for worship, and helps them find seating. The *GIFTS* needed: a friendly disposition with an outgoing and sincere personality.

    MY RESPONSE: YES _____ MAYBE _____ NO _____

Steps to Discipleship

The gift of understanding can lead to a new spiritual awakening for ourselves and the people around us. Take the following phrases, which come from Ephesians 4.17-24, and write what you think each phrase means. Then suggest a way in which the phrase could be applied to a teenager's life.

got to do with me? What's that

You must no longer live as the pagans do — their minds empty, their understanding darkened.

MEANING _____

_____

APPLICATION_____

_____

_____

They [the pagans] are estranged from a life in God because of their ignorance and their resistance.

MEANING _____

_____

APPLICATION_____

_____

_____

Without remorse they have abandoned themselves to lust and the indulgence of every sort of lewd conduct.

MEANING _____

_____

APPLICATION_____

_____

_____

You must lay aside your former way of life and the old self which deteriorates through illusion and desire.

MEANING _____

_____

APPLICATION_____

_____

_____

Acquire a fresh, spiritual way of thinking.

MEANING _____

_____

APPLICATION_____

_____

_____

Put on that new man created in God's image, whose justice and holiness are born of truth.

MEANING _____

_____

APPLICATION_____

_____

_____

Chapter 9

The Powerful Gift of Wisdom

Melissa's Secret Is Discovered

"Just what do you think you are doing?" Melissa insisted.

Sally McIntyre jumped back from the desk drawer where Melissa kept some of her "private" belongings. Melissa stormed into the room and was now standing over Sally by the desk. Sally looked up at the blazing blue eyes and started to cry. Finally, the little girl managed to mumble, "I wasn't doing anything."

But the letters Melissa had received from Doug Jackson were spread out all across the desk. Doug was a high-school sophomore she had met three months before. Sally had been snooping! Melissa knew that Sally didn't read well enough to understand them, but these were personal letters! Not even Mark knew about them. Melissa got them secretly through Doug's younger brother at school. Doug wrote that she was the only girl he cared about. He kept asking Melissa to go steady with him. Melissa was still trying to find a way to meet with him without her parents' knowledge.

An hour later, Melissa was still angry, but she said nothing. At 10 o'clock on this Saturday morning, the twins and their dad, Dan McIntyre, were driving across town. Augustine had told his four friends about one of the older men he played horseshoes with. George Manzoni was eighty-four and lived alone. He needed help with some yard work, Augustine said. The twins' dad and Skip Hamilton, Jesse's father, had volunteered to help.

Augustine and George were already waiting for the clean-up crew. They were playing checkers on the porch when the McIntyres pulled up. Jesse, his dad, and Juanita pulled into the driveway a moment later.

What Does 'I Love You' Mean?

"Love you! Thanks for coming!" Augustine shouted, waving from the porch. Dressed in old faded jeans and a workshirt, Augustine seemed happy to be rescued from checkers. "It's too much for me," he admitted sheepishly. He introduced everyone to old George, who then went inside to fix an Italian lunch for later. Augustine showed Dan McIntyre and Skip Hamilton a dead tree that needed to be cut down. Jesse and Mark were assigned to the mower because the lawn was a foot high.

"Love you. . . ." Melissa turned those words over and over in her mind. She and Juanita were weeding in Mr. Manzoni's "flower" garden, but she really wasn't there. That was how Doug signed every letter — *Love you.* Would he ever say those special words to her in person? Melissa asked herself.

"What's — or should I say — who's on your mind?" Juanita finally asked Melissa.

The two had been pulling weeds by the handfuls. Melissa, usually a chatterbox, had been strangely quiet. Juanita had been joking, but she couldn't help seeing the quick blush on Melissa's cheeks. The silence continued until Melissa ran to get a small radio from her dad's car. Without another word being spoken, Juanita knew that her best friend was in love. Juanita didn't like it at all.

By 3:00 P.M., the yard of George Manzoni was neat and beautiful once again. Dan McIntyre and Skip Hamilton had even gone out to buy some flowers to plant in the flower beds. Under Augustine's direction, the twins, Jesse, and Juanita had them planted in no time. The old man stood on the porch with tears in his black eyes. The flowers, he said, reminded him of his wife, who had died ten years before.

"Anna would love them," he said, thanking them for the flowers.

Jesse's father and the twins' dad left the four in the middle of the afternoon. After good-byes to Mr. Manzoni, Augustine and his four friends headed for a frozen-yogurt shop. Augustine was treating. He also wanted to talk to them one last time about their upcoming Confirmation.

Loving With Wisdom

Soon they were all seated at a corner table covered with a red-checked tablecloth. Large color posters of entertainment celebrities and a few famous animals were hanging on the walls. They were all eating the house specialty — yogurt. Juanita and Melissa kidded Mark about his resemblance to a chimpanzee eating yogurt on the poster right behind him.

"I can't believe that this is such healthy food!" Augustine exclaimed. "It's so delicious!"

'Shouldn't the things we love be good for us?'

"Yeah," laughed Mark, shoveling a spoonful of blueberry yogurt into his mouth. "Except for yogurt, it seems like the things I love aren't any good for me. And the things I don't love — like liver and lima beans — are supposed to be so good!"

"Augustine, why is that?" Melissa asked in a serious tone. "Shouldn't the things and the people we really love be good for us?"

Augustine smiled and ran his long, thin hand through his white hair. He turned to his fascinating, dark-haired, blue-eyed friend. For a moment, he remembered his own wild youth and the struggles he had had learning how to love properly. When Melissa looked into his eyes, she had an uncomfortable feeling. It was as though he knew of her difficulties of the heart.

"We all have trouble learning to love with wisdom," Augustine said. "But you're right, Melissa. There is something wrong with reality now, but God didn't plan it that way. In the garden of Eden, Adam and Eve loved only what was good and what was good for them. But then, the two sinned. They lost that natural ability to love with wisdom, and we inherit that shortcoming."

"I suppose that means that I should love liver!" Mark joked, finishing his last spoonful of frozen yogurt with relish.

"Maybe liver yogurt would be your answer!" laughed Augustine.

"Pffhewtt!" Mark sputtered dramatically. He started to act just as though he had something awful, something poisonous, in his mouth. As everyone laughed at Mark's antics, Jesse leaned over and patted his coughing friend on the back.

"Easy, fella," Jesse reassured Mark.

"You all remember," Augustine said a moment later, "that we have talked about the gifts of the Holy Spirit as gifts of power. You have learned that these gifts will be renewed and strengthened in you at Confirmation.

This gift of wisdom is the last one that we must talk about. It is a wonderful gift, and it has a lot to do with love.

"True wisdom, the Church tells us," Augustine continued, "shows us what God wants us to do — how to judge between good and evil, and how to make judgments about everything in our lives based on God's love. That's why Jesus knew when to begin his ministry. That's why he could judge when the time was right to go to Jerusalem to be crucified. But Jesus couldn't have had wisdom without this tremendous union of love with his Father and the Holy Spirit.

"St. James said that 'wisdom from above . . . is first of all innocent. It is also peaceable, lenient, docile, rich in sympathy and the kindly deeds that are its fruits, impartial and sincere.'[1] Worldly wisdom, on the other hand," Augustine said, "is 'devilish, cunning.' I think you know the words *wise guy* and *wisecrack,* and I'll bet you know the kind of 'wisdom' they represent."

"Yeah," agreed Jesse, nodding his head, "I know a few wise guys that ain't so wise."

"You should," commented Mark, looking Jesse in the eye until Jesse began to laugh.

"Well," smiled Augustine, "I'm sure that St. James must have known a few wise guys in Galilee too. But he also had a chance to see a man really filled with the gift of wisdom. James was an Apostle. He lived and traveled with Jesus for three years."

"But Jesus didn't really need wisdom, did he," offered Juanita. "I mean he was already God." Juanita had been eating her frozen peach yogurt a little too slowly. Now, it was a pale pink swirl in the bottom of her dish.

"Yes, he was God," admitted Augustine. "But he was also fully man. St. Luke says that the boy Jesus 'progressed steadily in wisdom and age and grace before God and men.'[2] In other words, he had to grow in wisdom, not as God but as man, in his human mind and heart. And he did that by growing in love. Jesus knew he was the *only* Son of God, and so he knew he was God. But he learned from experience how to put his love into practice every day of his life. There are examples of this all through the Gospels."

"I liked the story about the woman who'd been committing adultery," interrupted Melissa. "The other Jews were going to stone her to death, which was the law. But Jesus told them that only those who had never sinned should stone her. They all left without lifting a pebble! That was really wise of Jesus!"

"But the wisdom came from his love," said Augustine, nodding to Melissa, "the kind of love that is more concerned about others than about self, the kind of love that is humble. That's what gives wisdom its ability to see clearly. The proud person in love with self is incapable of wisdom. That was the real message of Jesus," added Augustine. "He tried to show that love was the great secret. 'You shall love the Lord your God with your whole heart, with your whole soul and with all your mind. You shall love your neighbor as yourself.'[3] Jesus said that those were the two 'great' commandments."

A Bitter Pill for Melissa

"Excuse me, sir, but talk about loving your neighbor!" chuckled Mark. "There's Doug Jackson with his latest neighbor. One of the guys on the basketball team told me that he has a new girl every week."

A tall, handsome, blond-haired boy had just walked up to the counter with a pretty red-haired girl dressed in a cheerleader's uniform. The girl was laughing at Doug because he seemed to be unable to decide on a flavor he wanted. "Oh, Doug!" she giggled.

Before anyone at the table realized it, Melissa jumped up from the chair she was sitting on. With a wild look in her eyes, with a face gone pale, she stomped across the room to the counter.

"So I'm the only girl you want to date, huh!" Melissa screamed at the shocked boy. "You said you wanted to go steady with me! You sent me all those letters. You creep!"

Slowly, the red-faced young man backed away from Melissa and signaled the girl to do the same. Silently, he tossed some money onto the counter and grabbed the two yogurts as Melissa glared at him. In a moment, Doug and the cheerleader were out the door. Melissa, on the other hand, was standing in the middle of the frozen-yogurt shop. She shut her eyes and stood there, trembling, fighting back the tears.

"Come on, 'Lissa, let's sit down."

Juanita had gone over to her best friend to lead her back to the table. Melissa had come willingly, rubbing away tears from her cheeks. She sat down, but no one had a thing to say to her. The only sound at this corner table was Melissa, sniffing.

"I didn't know anything about this, but I'm really

sorry he hurt your feelings, Sis." Mark said finally. "I'll go beat him up if you want me to."

"Naw, I'll go," insisted Jesse. "He's more my size."

"He said he loved me," whined Melissa, her face in a tissue. "I'm so embarrassed. He was just sending me those letters every week. He never meant a word about how much he liked me."

Suddenly, Augustine, who was sitting right next to Melissa, wrapped his arm around her shoulders. As he pulled her, chair and all, closer to him, the sound of Melissa's chair scraping against the wood floor made her friends laugh. Not ready to laugh, Melissa turned her head and pushed it into Augustine's jacket. It still carried the scent of leaves he had helped them rake and a rich piney smell from the trees at Mr. Manzoni's. She had grown to love this gentle and wise man.

Augustine's Last Lesson

"I know this is painful for Melissa, but I think it provides us with a good lesson about wisdom and love," said Augustine softly. With her head still against his jacket, Melissa could feel Augustine's words vibrat-

ing within his chest. She felt the anger, the quick burn of shame leaving her.

"Ecclesiastes says, 'in much wisdom there is much sorrow.'⁴ But it is St. Paul in his first letter to the Corinthians, the Christians of Corinth in Greece, who gives us a much better look at what love means," said Augustine, continuing. "Believe me, every Christian needs to think about what Paul says about love once in a while. I know I did!" Melissa sat up straight now and looked at this mysterious man who claimed to come from the ancient world with the blessings of God.

"First of all, Paul said that 'love is patient,' " Augustine said, smiling at Melissa. "Then, Paul said 'love is kind. Love is not jealous, it does not put on airs, it is not snobbish.' He went on to remind the Corinthians that 'love is never rude, it is not self-seeking, it is not prone to anger; neither does it brood over injuries.' "⁵

"I know that Doug wasn't loving me in those ways," Melissa admitted quietly. "And I guess I was pretty jealous and rude and angry to him."

"We understand, Melissa," Augustine said, reassuring her. "But Paul

also said that 'love does not rejoice in what is wrong but rejoices with the truth. There is no limit to love's forbearance, to its trust, its hope, its power to endure.' "⁶

"Oh, boy! That makes it pretty tough to love with wisdom!" Melissa complained. A touch of the old fire, the old Melissa was back.

"But you have a lifetime to learn," laughed Augustine, "and the gift of wisdom will strengthen you. But you know, I think I need a little strengthening right now."

All four looked at him with blank expressions.

"How about another round of frozen yogurt?" suggested Augustine. "After all, we all love it, and it's good for us!"

The girl behind the counter noticed that the corner table with the four young people and the old gentlemen was a bit unruly, a bit too loud once again. She went over to settle the group down. One "scene" in the place was quite enough for the afternoon.

---

¹ James 3.17. ² Luke 2.52.
³ Matthew 22.37,39.
⁴ Ecclesiastes 1.18.
⁵ 1 Corinthians 13.4-5 ⁶ *Ibid.,* 13.6-7.

A Young Teen's Book of Catholic Knowledge

1. **What does the gift of wisdom empower us to do?**

    The gift of wisdom helps us to distinguish between what is good and what is evil as well as to make judgments about everything in our lives based on God's love.

2. **What is "wisdom from above"?**

    It is the wisdom of God given through the Holy Spirit.

3. **What is the difference between worldly wisdom and "wisdom from above"?**

    Worldly wisdom does not take spiritual values into account, and so can be self-centered and cunning. The proud person in love with self is incapable of wisdom. "Wisdom from above" helps sincere Christians decide what they should do and how they can be helpful to others.

4. **What is the wisdom that God sends that we should know?**

    The wisdom all people should know is the message of the Cross — that Christ died for our sins and rose again so that we might have everlasting life.

5. **How do we know God's wisdom?**

    We can receive the gift of wisdom from the Holy Spirit. The gift of wisdom is also given to the Church to teach and protect the truth revealed by God.

6. **What is the foundation of wisdom?**

    The love that is modeled for us by Jesus.

7. **What are the two "great" commandments given by Jesus?**

    You shall love the Lord your God with your whole heart, with your whole soul, and with all your mind. You shall love your neighbor as yourself.

8. **How does St. Paul describe Christian love?**

    Love is patient, kind, not jealous. Love does not put on airs and is not snobbish. Love is not rude or self-seeking. Love is not prone to anger and doesn't brood over injuries. Love is gladdened by the truth and saddened by wrong.

9. **Does Jesus show us how to love?**

    Yes, he lived love by his actions — by forgiving and not passing rash judgment, by being firm when he had to be, by showing compassion to the suffering, by being sensitive to human needs, and by helping others.

St. Francis of Assisi

He was born in 1182 in Assisi, Italy, while his father was in France on business. When Pietro (Peter) di Bernardone came home to find a new son, he named him Francesco (Francis) after the country where he had been traveling. The Bernardones were wealthy, and Francis grew up enjoying beautiful clothes and all the fun money could buy.

Like many young men in this century, he believed that war was glorious. At nineteen, the young Bernardone became a soldier. He fought in a small war between Assisi and a neighboring city, Perugia. But Francis was captured and in prison for a year. Not long after he was freed, he became very ill and almost died. Those two experiences somehow made him feel different about life.

Nevertheless, when he was well, he prepared to go to war again. His father bought him the finest horse, armor, and weapons anyone in Assisi had ever seen. But on the day that Francis rode out of Assisi, he met a sad, poorly dressed soldier along the road. Francis was touched by the sight. He gave his fine clothes to the poor soldier and wore the other's rags instead. Another day, Francis was praying in a rundown church named San Damiano.

"Francis," a voice said, "don't you see that my house is falling down? Go and build it up."

Francis knew that it was the voice of God. He sold his horse and also some cloth to get money to repair the church.

The little church of the Porziuncola in the valley below Assisi, where St. Francis established his order's headquarters, is preserved within the larger church of Our Lady of the Angels.

Later, Francis had the wisdom to see that God was really asking him to rebuild his Church by founding a religious order.

After that, people in Assisi noticed a great change in the young man. He wanted to give his life to God, not soldiering. He also understood that he had to leave behind a life he once loved.

Some people wondered if his moodiness meant that he was in love. Francis said he was and that he wanted to "marry" Lady Poverty. He was seen giving his money to beggars on the way to Rome.

Pietro di Bernardone was angry that Francis was wasting money and acting foolishly. He expected his son to appreciate the good things he had given him. A showdown between father and son finally took place in front of the bishop. Francis gave everything he had back to his father, including his clothes. From then on, he said, he would be truly poor. He had a wisdom that was beyond the world's concern with money and power.

Other men came to join Francis. Francis called them "Friars Minor," or the "Little Brothers." Later on, this order and another order he founded for women were called "Franciscans." A wonderful development was the Franciscan Third Order, for lay people who live in the world as secular Franciscans. They all accepted poverty in order to grow closer to God and to give to the poor. But they were very joyful about their poverty. Francis saw the wealth of God's love in animals, fish, birds — all of nature. So, he composed poems and songs out of his love for God. A very famous one is called the "Canticle of the Sun."

In 1224, Francis miraculously received the same wounds Jesus suffered in crucifixion. In humility, Francis then bandaged his hands and feet to hide the nail holes. But the wounds and his hard way of life weakened him. Welcoming "Sister Death," he died praising God in 1226 at the age of forty-four. In recognition of his great virtue, he was canonized just four years later in 1230. By almost any standard, St. Francis of Assisi is seen as one of the greatest followers of Jesus in the Church.

Photos by Rev. Patrick McSherry, O.F.M. Cap.

A fresco believed to be a good likeness of St. Francis is found in the Basilica named after him. In a chapel crypt, his remains are kept.

How Are You Growing in Christian Love?

St. Paul, in 1 Corinthians 13, speaks of love as the way that surpasses all others. He said: "If I speak with human tongues and angelic as well, but do not have love, I am a noisy gong, a clanging cymbal." He also said: "If I have faith great enough to move mountains, but have not love, I am nothing." And: "If I give everything I have to feed the poor . . . but have not love, I gain nothing."

How are you growing in Christian love? On a scale of one to 10, rank yourself on the following qualities that St. Paul uses to describe love. A "1" indicates need for much growth. A "10" indicates that you have arrived (but don't lose it). Write your number in the boxes provided.

☐ **Patient:** I am not hasty in reacting when I don't get something I want. I react calmly to disappointments and don't sulk or complain when I don't get my way.

☐ **Kind:** I am sympathetic to other people's needs and am ready to help them whenever I can. I am gentle in the way I treat people and considerate in respecting their feelings.

☐ **Not Jealous:** I am not intolerant or distrustful of others just because they want something I want. I don't envy others or feel bitterness toward them because of their success.

☐ **Does Not Put On Airs:** I'm not putting on an act to impress others. I don't try to fool others about the things I have and the things I do.

☐ **Not Snobbish:** I don't act as though I'm superior to other people. I don't look down on others just because they may come from poor families or because their parents don't have prestigious jobs.

☐ **Never Rude:** I am not mean or discourteous to others. I do not speak or act in crude or offensive ways with others. I don't treat others as if they were unimportant.

☐ **Not Self-seeking:** I don't think just of myself or always put myself first. I am generous in giving my time and talent to others for their sake, not to win praise for myself.

☐ **Not Prone to Anger:** I don't get enraged when I don't get my way. I do not feel hatred or resentment toward others or seek ways of hurting them.

☐ **Does Not Brood Over Injuries:** I don't whine and moan and sulk when I am ignored or insulted. I do not try to think of ways of getting revenge when someone wrongs me.

☐ **Does Not Rejoice in What Is Wrong But Rejoices in the Truth:** I am not glad when people I don't like are punished for something they didn't do. I do not participate in malicious gossip, backbiting, or slander. I am happy when people are treated fairly and justly.

Steps to Discipleship

Let us love one another
because love is of God;
everyone who loves is begotten of God
and has knowledge of God.
The man without love has known nothing
of God, for God is love (1 John 4.7-8).

Let us create, beginning on paper, a world of love. Take each aspect of love and suggest some thought or action that would show growth in it. Put no limit on your imagination. Think in terms of your home, school, community, nation, or the world. For example:

Love is patient. *I will be more respectful of my parents when they say I'm too young to do something I would like to do.*

Love is kind.

Love is not jealous.

Love does not put on airs.

Love is not snobbish.

Love is never rude.

Love is not self-seeking.

Love is not prone to anger.

Love does not brood over injuries.

Love does not rejoice in what is wrong but rejoices in the truth.

Chapter 10

Do Not Stifle the Spirit

Getting-Ready Memories

Melissa swung around once again in front of the full-length mirror in the McIntyres' one and only upstairs bathroom. The new baby-blue dress she had picked out with her mother the week before did have a nice flair, she had to admit. She had wanted a flowered orange dress that was more "dramatic." But her mother had held out for a dress that was less "showy" for her Confirmation.

" 'Lissa, can I come in?" Sally was outside the bathroom door again, begging to come in. Her little sister loved to watch Melissa get dressed up. But Melissa was always careful not to let Sally in while she was putting on makeup. She didn't want to give Sally ideas that could lead to "experimenting" when she wasn't around. But Sally soon settled on the side of the tub to watch Melissa combing her hair.

"Melissa, your head won't catch on fire will it?" Sally asked suddenly.

"What?" Melissa exclaimed, swinging around to look at Sally. Sally's blue eyes, she noticed, were filled with concern.

"I was looking at the 'firmation book you and Mark use," Sally explained. "There was a picture of the Apostles, and their heads were all on fire. Mom said it was going to happen to you and to Mark tonight."

Melissa collapsed with laughter and sat down hard next to Sally on the tub.

"No, Sal," Melissa explained, patting Sally's cheek, "we aren't going to catch on fire! I think you really knew that! What will happen is that Mark and I and all the other kids being confirmed will receive a kind of fire on the inside. But of course, it won't hurt. It will be the Holy Spirit."

"Will you feel it?" Sally continued.

Melissa looked down into her kid sister's upturned face framed by soft blond hair like their Dad's. Most of the time, she enjoyed having a little sister. "I hope so . . ." Melissa said. "I really do hope so."

On the other side of the bathroom door, Mark had begun to pound. "Girls! Girls!" he said in his most sarcastic tone. "I want to be confirmed tonight! Let's go!"

Melissa had checked out her hair "one last time." Fifteen minutes later, the McIntyre family was getting out of the car in the parking lot far below the tall Gothic spires of St. Ignatius. Mark and Melissa hurried over to the parish hall. Grandpa Foster had been so pleased and proud when Mark asked him to be his Confirmation sponsor. The doctors had been surprised to see how well Jack Foster had recovered after his heart attack. But to spare him extra walking, Grandpa Foster was driven up to the door of the hall where sponsors and candidates were supposed to gather before going into church.

"Did you call Augustine to tell him that Confirmation was going to be earlier?" Mark asked Jesse. The four friends and the other candidates were now lining up with their teachers and sponsors.

"Oh, I forgot!" exclaimed Jesse, slapping his forehead with disgust.

"Oh no!" exclaimed Melissa who was standing nearby with Aunt Margie. Right behind Melissa were Juanita and her sponsor.

"Oh, don't worry. He'll be there," reasoned Aunt

Margie, who was Melissa's sponsor. It was too late anyway. A heaviness, a sharp sense of letdown, had fallen across these four. They had been waiting for this very special day. The line had already begun to move. There was no time to phone their great friend and teacher, Augustine.

Augustine Reminisces

Old St. Ignatius was crowded but hushed. Candles blazed on all of the altars. Bright red banners with tongues of fire and symbols of the Holy Spirit had been hung with great effort on either side of the altar. Flower arrangements in red and white were set around the sanctuary and near the bishop's chair. In the choir loft, the organ began to play softly.

Though the church was filling, an older dark-complected man in a dark pinstriped suit spotted an empty pew off the middle aisle. Augustine knelt down right next to the aisle. His eyes closed tightly, and a wonderful light seemed to spread across the strong face. He rested his head in his hands and simply talked to the Lord he had learned

to love so long ago, so very long ago.

But then, his mind was flooded with memories of the four young people he'd come to guide. He smiled through his fingers. He couldn't help remembering their worried faces at the old Bentley house as they eyed a stranger in a hallway where ghosts were said to wander. *Nomen meum est*

Aurelius Augustinus, he'd said in introducing himself there. Melissa's eyes had grown so wide at the sound of such fancy language.

That was the first time he'd taught them. He told them that they would receive power, a surge of God's love and strength, when they received the Holy Spirit in Confirmation. Later, his great role as teacher seemed to mean very little in the park. Young Mark had knocked him down! Him! Augustine! Bishop of Hippo and Doctor of the Church! Bowled over by a boy! Augustine laughed quietly to himself. They had talked about conversion that day. The word had taken on some flesh and blood. And yet, these youngsters had still been concerned that friends at school would think them weird if they were to really act like disciples of Jesus!

But their hearts and spirits had grown! A birthday party, a car wash, a hospital for the handicapped, an ice-cream shop. Strange places to learn about wonder and awe, reverence, courage, right judgment, knowledge, understanding, and wisdom! But the Lord always had his wisdom about these things.

The strains of organ music were now thunderous in Augustine's ears. He raised his head up out of his hands and looked around. The McIntyres had moved into his pew just to the left of him. Sally McIntyre waved at him shyly. When she was sure of herself, she slid down the pew next to him.

All Her Houses Shall Cry Out, Alleluia!

The procession of young candidates and their sponsors was beginning in front of the bishop. The congregation rose to its feet and began to sing.
"Come Holy Spirit, and fill our hearts . . .
Thank you, Jesus, for loving us . . .
Thank you, Jesus, for setting us free . . .
Thank you, Jesus, for being here . . .

'Today the Spirit will come upon them in power.'

Alleluia! Alleluia! Alleluia!"
They were four lively verses "foreign" to Augustine's fifth-century ear, but the enthusiasm appealed to him. And the simple lyrics were flawless.

The double rows of youngsters to be confirmed filed past. Sally slipped around him to stand at the edge of the pew for a better view. But Augustine knew that, through the grace of God, he had the best "view" in the church. He "felt" the moment his four young friends were moving past. He turned and looked right into the upturned face of Melissa McIntyre.

"You're here!" she gasped with delight. But

Augustine only winked and smiled at the dark-haired girl in the new baby-blue dress.

Right behind Melissa came Jesse, whose face was still downcast. Augustine reached out and tapped the young man's shoulder. In a second, the boy moved past, but Augustine knew that Jesse had left a heavy spirit, a sense of embarrassment, behind him. Juanita and Mark were in the procession line at the other side of the aisle. But they had seen him. Mark smiled broadly at Augustine, at his parents, and at Sally. At the front, the candidates filed into the pews with their sponsors. Jack Foster moved into a pew with his grandson Mark.

Introductory Rites

Finally, the procession was complete. A young, blond-haired bishop, Bishop Swanson, bowed in front of the altar, and turned to face the congregation at St. Ignatius. He gave his large wooden pastoral staff to Father Mike. His attendants took their places to the side of the flower-filled altar. "This is a special day, a holy day in the lives of these young people," insisted the young bishop. "Today, the Holy Spirit will come upon them in power, strengthening them to be disciples of Jesus. Let us pray that they will not stifle the Spirit."

Then the penitential rite of the Mass began. "As we prepare to celebrate the mystery of Christ's love," the bishop told the people, "let us acknowledge our failures and ask the Lord for pardon and strength." Sitting close to the front, Jesse Hamilton was struck by those words. He knew that those words meant more to him now than they once did. Augustine had taught him that it took courage to admit a mistake and to reform your life.

"Lord, fulfill your promise," Bishop Swanson prayed. "Send your Holy Spirit to make us witnesses before the world to the Good News proclaimed by Jesus Christ our Lord, who lives and reigns with you and the Holy Spirit, one God, for ever and ever."

Presentation of the Candidates

After the Liturgy of the Word, the bishop took his seat, and Father Mike went to the lectern to announce the candidates. Earlier that day, the pastor had prayed earnestly that all would go smoothly — that the participants in the liturgy would come prepared, the microphones work, the confirmands respond appropriately to the solemn occasion, and that the bishop would arrive before it was time to get nervous. Now he beamed with pride as he began to announce the names of the confirmands — Abigail Barnhart, Cynthia Connelly, John Davidson, James Young — and they stood to signify their readiness.

Homily or Instruction

Then the celebrant stepped up to the lectern to begin the homily. He had taken off the tall miter and began to speak. "He looks much too young to be a bishop," Augustine thought to himself. He himself had been forty-one when named bishop of Hippo. "I suppose everyone should look young to me now," Augustine smiled to himself.

Bishop Swanson spoke about Confirmation in the early days of the Church. He had a soft sort of voice, but he spoke with such feeling. "When St. Paul placed his hands on those who had been baptized, the Holy Spirit came upon them," he said. "They began to speak in other languages and in prophetic words. In our day, the coming of the Holy Spir-

it in Confirmation is no longer marked by the gift of tongues, but we know his coming by faith. He fills our hearts with the love of God, brings us together in one faith but in different vocations, and works within us to make the Church one and holy."

The bishop reminded them: "You have already been baptized into Christ, and now you will receive the power and grace of his Spirit, and the sign of the cross on your forehead. You must be witnesses before all the world to his life, especially to his suffering, death, and resurrection; your way of life should at all times reflect the goodness of Christ."

Renewal of Baptismal Promises

When the bishop had stepped to the center once again, the candidates stood to renew the profession of faith made at Baptism.

"Do you reject Satan and all his works and all his empty promises?" the bishop asked.

"I do," the candidates responded in unison.

"Do you believe in God, the Father almighty, creator of heaven and earth?"

"I do."

"Do you believe in Jesus

Christ, his only Son, our Lord, who was born of the Virgin Mary, was crucified, died, and was buried, rose from the dead, and is now seated the right hand of the Father?"

"I do."

"Do you believe in the Holy Spirit, the Lord, the giver of life, who came upon the Apostles at Pentecost and today is given to you sacramentally in Confirmation?"

"I do."

"Do you believe in the holy catholic Church, the communion of saints, the forgiveness of sins, the resurrection of the body, and life everlasting?"

"I do."

"This is our faith," the bishop concluded. "This is the faith of the Church. We are proud to profess it in Christ Jesus our Lord."

As the organ played, the candidates filed out of their pews and lined up in front of the altar. The bishop was to lay hands upon each one just as Peter and Paul had laid hands upon believers in the first century.

The Laying On of Hands

"My dear friends," Bishop Swanson said in a voice that seemed to be stronger as the Mass continued. "In Baptism, God our Father gave the new birth of eternal life to his chosen sons and daughters. Let us pray to our Father that he will pour out the Holy Spirit to strengthen his sons and daughters with his gifts and anoint them to be more like Christ the Son of God."

With the pastor holding his bishop's staff, Bishop Swanson extended his hands over the candidates. Not at all sure what was going on, Sally climbed into Augustine's lap for a aisle-side view. The bishop prayed: "All-powerful God, Father of our Lord Jesus Christ, by water and the Holy Spirit you freed your sons and daughters from sin and gave them new life. Send your Holy Spirit upon them to be their Helper and Guide. Give them the spirit of wisdom and understanding, the spirit of right judgment and courage, the spirit of knowledge and reverence. Fill them with the spirit of wonder and awe in your presence. We ask this through Christ our Lord."

"Amen," the candidates responded. Those gifts of the Holy Spirit had a new meaning, especially to Mark, Melissa, Jesse, and Juanita. Just like the ancient Hebrews and early Christians, they said the "amen" as if they felt the power of its meaning: Yes, it is true!

The Anointing With Chrism

When that was concluded, each sponsor took a place behind the candidates and placed a hand on the right shoulder of the candidate. Sally grinned when she saw her grandfather rise and walk to Mark.

Slowly, Bishop Swanson moved again down the line. Father Mike and several altar boys accompanied him. One by one, each sponsor spoke the name that the candidate had chosen as a Confirmation name. Then, the bishop dipped his right thumb into a small glass dish that Father Mike was holding. With this chrism, a mixture of olive oil and balsam blessed by the bishop, Bishop Swanson then made a cross on the forehead of each one.

"Robert, be sealed with the Gift of the Holy Spirit," Bishop Swanson said to Greg Schwartz, who was standing next to Mark.

With the action of the anointing on the forehead and with those words, the Sacrament of Confirmation was conferred. Through the action and words of the bishop, Christ had confirmed and strengthened the young people in the Holy Spirit.

"Amen," Greg responded.

"Peace be with you," the bishop continued.

"And also with you," Greg said.

"Augustine!" Mark said proudly looking up into the face of Bishop Swanson. The blue eyes seemed to smile. But suddenly, time seemed to stand still. As he watched, Bishop Swanson's fair face fringed with blond hair seemed to fade into thin air. Suddenly, a taller, more muscular man with a dark complexion and white hair seemed to be standing there in a sort of mist.

Mark closed his eyes, shook his head and looked up again. He couldn't believe his eyes and yet. . . . There in front of him stood Augustine in bishop's robes, holding a staff that seemed to be rough cut from a tree. The clothing, Mark noticed, was different too. It was simple, hand-sewn, but beautiful. Mark's eyes searched for the face, and suddenly the mist dissolved. The eyes he knew so well were now looking straight at him. They were laughing at him, but there was love in the laugh.

Augustine raised his hand to bless him, and Mark felt a strange stirring deep in his spirit. But just as suddenly as the vision had appeared, it was gone. Mark shook his head again and swallowed hard. He felt Grandpa Foster's hand tighten on his shoulder. He looked up to see Father Mike eyeing him with curiosity. Bishop Swanson moved on to confirm the girl next to him. "Ann," responded Claire Cunningham.

In a little while, general intercessions of the Mass were read. "God, our Father," Bishop Swanson concluded, "you sent your Holy Spirit upon the Apostles, and through them and their successors, you give the Spirit to your people. May his work begun at Pentecost continue to grow in the hearts of all who believe. We ask this through Christ our Lord."

From then, the Mass of Confirmation seemed to go too quickly. The Liturgy of the Eucharist had never been more beautiful, Juanita thought. Something special had happened to her during this liturgy. She had been fed with the Body and Blood of her Lord. Juanita felt a newness in her as she knew that the Savior was not just the Lord, but *her* Lord. The bishop had talked about how it was really Christ who conferred this sacrament and about their hearts being on fire with

109

love, and she thought maybe she knew what that meant.

"God our Father . . ." The bishop was saying the final blessing, and the newly confirmed were filled with the sense that they really had been blessed in a special way. "Complete the work you have begun and keep the gifts of your Holy Spirit active in the hearts of your people," prayed Bishop Swanson. "Make them ready to live his Gospel and eager to do his will. May they never be ashamed to proclaim to all the world Christ crucified living and reigning for ever and ever."

Signs and Wonders Shared

As the newly confirmed filed down the main aisle in front of the bishop a few moments later, the church almost seemed to shake with music. Mark knew he was supposed to keep his eyes straight in front of him, but he couldn't help himself. As he passed the pew where his family was sitting, he turned to his right. There he spotted Augustine. He was sure they were the same eyes that looked at him only moments ago at the altar. They were smiling at him again. Had it been his imagina-tion? What had happened?

"Guess what?" Mark grabbed Jesse's arm as the two broke ranks on the steps of St. Ignatius. The newly confirmed were to go to the parish hall where families and guests were soon gathering to meet the bishop. Grandpa Foster had waited inside to walk over with his daughter and son-in-law. "Something happened to me during Confirmation!" Mark told Jesse.

'Mark felt a strange stirring deep in his spirit.'

Jesse had never heard Mark sound so excited, so . . . mysterious.

Mark grabbed his friend by the shoulders and moved him over to the side. He told Jesse how he had seemed to see Augustine the way he was as a bishop. "It was as if I was in a whole other place and time."

"Far out!" Jesse exclaimed. "Can't say that happened to me, but in my heart, I know I got the Spirit."

The two laughed to each other and began to walk toward the parish hall. They wondered what Melissa and Juanita had experienced.

But they knew that they wouldn't find Augustine among the guests at St. Ignatius Hall. It was the end of a story but a continuation too. All four had read the lines in the Acts of the Apostles that Peter had quoted from the prophet Joel. Now, on this day of Confirmation, they took on a new, a powerful meaning.

"It shall come to pass in
    the last days, says
    God,
that I will pour out a por-
    tion of my spirit on all
    mankind:
Your sons and daughters
    shall prophesy,
your young men shall see
    visions and your old
    men shall dream
    dreams.
Yes, even on my servants
    and handmaids
I will pour out a portion of
    my spirit in those
    days,
and they shall prophesy.
I will work wonders in
    the heavens above
and signs on the earth
    below."[1]

[1] Acts 2.17-19.

A Young Teen's Book of Catholic Knowledge

1. **What effects take place in receiving the Sacrament of Confirmation?**
   We are strengthened in the Holy Spirit by a pouring in of God's love and power into our souls, which we call grace. The Church has always taught that the presence of this grace of the sacrament actually makes a permanent sign, or character, on our souls.

2. **Are the effects of this sacrament produced automatically?**
   No. For a sacrament to be effective, the mind and heart of the receiver must be open to the will of Christ and the teaching of the Church.

3. **When did we first receive the Holy Spirit?**
   In Baptism

4. **What does our Confirmation call us to witness?**
   We must be witnesses of Christ's life, especially of his suffering, death, and resurrection.

5. **What should our way of life reflect?**
   The goodness of Christ.

6. **By what action is the Sacrament of Confirmation conferred?**
   Through the anointing with chrism on the forehead, which is done by the imposition of the hand.

7. **What are the words used in conferring the sacrament?**
   (Name), be sealed with the Gift of the Holy Spirit.

8. **Who actually does the confirming in the Sacrament of Confirmation?**
   Christ confirms or strengthens us in the Holy Spirit. The bishop is Christ's minister, or instrument, for the sacrament. He is called the ordinary minister. A priest can confirm a parishioner in danger of death, and can also confirm in ceremonies of Christian initiation. In such cases, a priest is called an extraordinary minister of Confirmation.

9. **Is it necessary that we "feel" something through our senses when we are confirmed?**
   Quite often people do not feel anything happen to them at Confirmation because God comes to them quietly and deeply. If a person does feel something, that is good; if not, that is good. What is important is that we entrust our lives to the Lord in faith. God will act in our lives whether we sensibly feel it or not.

Steps to Discipleship

This concluding chapter sets out a basic plan for Catholic living. If you follow this plan, you will be able to live according to the commands of Christ and his Church, and grow in spiritual maturity. It is important to remember that the Sacrament of Confirmation is a sacrament of initiation. It is not an end but the beginning of a new life in Christ.

- Imitate Jesus Christ in your thoughts and actions in all of life's situations.

- Witness your faith in Jesus Christ to others when you have the opportunity.

- Attend Mass faithfully on Sundays and Holy Days and participate as fully as possible. Try to attend daily Mass at least occasionally.

- Pray personally every day and grow in your prayer life.

- Be supportive and helpful to your parents, and be ready to forgive them when they err.

- Develop a servant's heart by helping, when you can, those in need or those who are hurting.

- Avoid mortal sin and the occasion of sin. When tempted toward sinful behavior, call upon Jesus to give you strength and courage to avoid sin. Avoid the situations that diminish rather than upbuild you or others.

- Celebrate the Sacrament of Reconciliation regularly, monthly if possible.

- Respect the teaching authority of the Church by thinking about and obeying the teachings of the Pope and the bishops.

- Encourage your pastor and others in authority in your parish.

- Love the Catholic Church and build up your own parish family.

- Put those things in your life that encourage faith and hope, peace and joy.

Memorize the following verses and always keep them in your mind and heart.

- "God so loved the world that he gave his only Son, that whoever believes in him may not die but may have eternal life" (John 3.16).

- "You shall love the Lord your God with all your heart, with all your soul, with all your strength, and with all your mind; and your neighbor as yourself" (Luke 10.27).